# Labouring Beside Lough Erne

## A Study of the Fermanagh Labour Movement, 1826-1932

### *Jim Quinn*

*Fermanagh Council of Trade Unions*
*A Centenary Publication 2019*

Umiskin Press

Grant Stream– Remembering
and Commemoration –
Decade of Centenaries

Fermanagh & Omagh
District Council
Comhairle Ceantair
Fhear Manach agus na hÓmaí

ISBN 978-1-9164489-2-6

Typeset in 10.5pt New Baskerville on 12.5 body.

Layout and Printing by
CRM Design + Print Ltd
Dublin 12

Produced by trade union labour in Ireland

Permission to reproduce copyright material is gratefully acknowledged.
Every effort has been made to trace copyright holders but if any have been inadvertently
overlooked the necessary arrangements will be made at the first opportunity

# Contents

The three cubs with Jim Brown, 2 April 1980

# Dedication

I would like to dedicate this publication to four Fermanagh comrades. First, the late James 'Jim' Brown (1924-2003). Jim was local Branch Secretary of the Transport & General Workers' Union (TGWU) in Enniskillen for half a century and Chair of Fermanagh Council of Trades Unions for nearly as long. He was a mentor and support to the many hundreds of members and Shop Stewards he helped. I first met Jim in the old Royal Hotel in Enniskillen when I joined the union in 1978. Jim encouraged me and two other young men to get more involved in the trade union and labour movement locally and to develop the skills and politics which allowed us to help thousands of people over the decades.

The others are Tommy Campbell who became involved around the same time in 1978 and Davy Kettyles after he returned from working as a Postman in London a short while later. Jim christened us 'the three cubs' at the time, a title we were delighted to have been given by a committed, compassionate socialist who learned his politics in the hiring fairs of Fermanagh and the horrors of the Second World War. Tommy went on to become a Regional Officer of Unite the Union in Aberdeen and Davy Kettyles is the Senior Organiser for Ireland of Unite's Organising and Leverage Department based in Belfast.

Jim Brown is never forgotten and his contribution will be recorded in the second part of our history as will that of my fourth comrade, the late Leo Monaghan who first persuaded me to be a 'temporary Shop Steward' in 1979. The rest, as they say, is history. We hope that a second publication will bring the local movement's history up to the present day. I know all of those honoured here would have been delighted to see this first part of our history being published in our Centenary year.

**Jim Quinn**

January 2019

# Umiskin Press, Ireland

**Umiskin Press** is a not-for-profit publishing house, publishing commissioned and non-commissioned works mainly, though not exclusively, works of labour history, Labour interest, trade union issues, poetry and cultural matters. Umiskin is a townland in Kilcar, County Donegal, birthplace of the McGinleys.

Dr. Kieran Jack McGinley is the principal behind Umiskin Press, whose recent publications were: *Left Lives in 20th Century Ireland*, Francis Devine & Kieran Jack McGinley, (October 2017*); Stephen McGonagle, Ombudsman, Trade Unionist, Senator,* Owen McGonagle (April 2018); *William Walker Centenary Essays* (October 2018) and *Left Lives 2,* upcoming, Spring 2019.

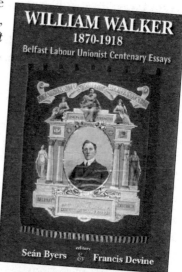

Umiskin Press is mainly interested in publishing limited runs of between 150 and 500 copies in hardback and paperback limited editions which might otherwise not merit commercial publication and sale elsewhere.

# Acknowledgements

I would like to thank the following for their assistance in the production of this publication. Firstly, my family and friends who must be sick of hearing about labour history in Fermanagh.

Secondly, I am indebted to those who assisted me in obtaining research information in the early days: Unite the Union (and its forerunner the TGWU); GMB Education Manchester; the ACE scheme researchers of Fermanagh Trades Council from the 1980s – Sylvia Donaldson, Vincent Breen, Malachy Mc Roe, and Ray Haydock; Anton Mc Cabe (Omagh) who was researching in a similar area when I started this journey over thirty years ago; staff in the *Fermanagh Herald Office* who are now mostly retired but they know who they are; staff in Enniskillen Library and in Ruskin College Library, Oxford, who allowed me to monopolise their Irish collection; and in recent times, staff of the Irish and Local History Library in Armagh whose radical paper archive will be very useful in our future research. Finally, I acknowledge my debt to my Ruskin College supervisor of the original thesis, Bob Purdie, who is sadly now deceased.

I would like to acknowledge the support of the current delegates and Officers of Fermanagh Council of Trades Unions for the production of this publication and for their support of other events in our Centenary year. Grateful thanks also to those who made this publication possible with their financial support through grants, donations and adverts: Fermanagh/ Omagh Council, Remembering and Commemoration – Decade of Centenaries Grant; ICTU Northern Ireland Committee; Unite the Union, Regional Office; Unite the Union Fermanagh Branch; Irish National Teachers' Organisation (INTO); Northern Ireland Public Service Alliance (NIPSA); MANDATE; CONNECT; Association of Secondary Teachers, Ireland (ASTI); SIPTU; Dublin Council of Trade Unions; Bray Council of Trades Union, Communication Workers' Union (CWU, Northern Ireland Branch) and Communication Workers' North West Branch.

I am grateful to the Jones family, Enniskillen, who gave additional information on John Jones; Marius Jones who kindly provided a photograph of his grandfather; Benny Cassidy (past Unison Rep and T&G member when I joined in 1978) and Old Enniskillen Facebook Page for use of his photographs; Pat D'Arcy who took images of sites around Enniskillen for this book when we first planned it many years ago; and

Frankie Roofe and Fermanagh Genealogy Centre who supplied information on the old streets and in particular some of those referenced here. Bernadette Layden, Jim Ledwith and the Crow's Nest Bar who gave pictures of the Jones and Kelly's Cottages Street signs.

Lastly, I want to thank Francis Devine (Irish Labour History Society) who planted this seed many decades ago and helped us to bring it to fruition in our Centenary year with Jack McGinley, Umiskin Press and Christy Hammond, CRM Design + Print Ltd., Dublin who have been so helpful throughout.

If I have left anyone out, I apologise in advance. If this book triggers any memories make sure to contact us and we will include the information in the second part of our history.

**Jim Quinn**

## Northern Ireland West Branch

### Congratulates Fermanagh Council of Trades Unions on its Centenary and looks forward to working with them for the next 100 years

# *Preface*

The primary sources used in this publication were local newspapers and the Executive minutes of the Irish Labour Party & Trades Union Congress (ILP&TUC), National Amalgamated Union of Labour (NAUL) and Transport & General Workers' Union (TGWU). These sources were relied upon in the absence of any surviving local union records for the period covered. A number of unions. in addition to the two mentioned above. were contacted but either had no records or did not reply. Primary sources were supplemented with information from published union histories, journal articles and other general works on Irish history. I have used this combination of sources to build a picture of Fermanagh's labour history from 1826 to 1934.

The history of the Fermanagh labour movement is one of workers' struggles for a decent life over nearly two centuries. Its advocates have come from across the community it represents. Over those centuries, a broad church of political opinion was involved in the local labour movement. While its main core were always firmly committed to its Labour/Socialist values, its activists at various times in its history reflected the community they were rooted and thus reflected Unionism, Nationalism, Orangeism, Republicanism and Communism.

However, throughout that time, the movement's core objective remained the organisation of workers of all views and none to defend and progress their interests. It has been buffeted by the turbulent history of our county from the Great Hunger to the Home Rule crisis, from the First World War, the 1916 Easter Rising, and Partition, right through to more recent times and crisis. In all of that time, it remained constant in its core objective to fight for a better life for ordinary women and men in our community, whether that was the building workers in 1826 setting a fair working week or Jones and Kelly fighting for decent housing in the Dardanelles.

This publication is being launched to commemorate the Centenary of Fermanagh Council of Trades Unions (FCTU), 1919-2019. It brings our history up to 1934. One obvious weakness in that record to date is the invisibility of women in the story of our movement locally. Women are mentioned in the activities of the teachers' unions, insurance workers, and in the struggle of the Lisbellaw Woollen factory workers. Women are mentioned almost as a novelty in a 1920 press report of a Labour Party meeting which talked of 'two women sitting in the front row' but there is no doubt that they will have been centrally involved in many of the industrial, political and community struggles recorded up to the 1930s, even if they weren't always visible.

In our next publication bringing our history to the 1970s and beyond, women will be much more visible within the local labour movement. They include people like the late Rosemary Stennett, first woman Secretary of FCTU; Máiréad Stewart, a local Shop Steward who carried out the same role for more than twenty years; and Jill Weir, current FCTU Vice-Chair and a long term activist in the NHS. They will be joined by people like Bunty Spillane who sat on the then FCTU in the early 70s; Shelly Marshall from the Communications Workers' Union who was active in the 1980s; and many other women who played their part in improving the lives of women and men in our county.

This publication does not attempt to give a deep political analysis of the history of our movement in Fermanagh. Rather it puts on record the struggle we have been involved in and remain involved in over the last two centuries. We hope it removes any cloak of invisibility which covered this part of our local history. We trust our work will assist future scholars and historians to delve further into that history.

**Ní Neart Go Cuir Le Chéile – Unity is Strength - Aye Strang Thegither**

# Introduction

As a trade union and socialist activist in Fermanagh for nearly forty years, it has always been frustrating to see how workers and their organisations have been largely written out of the history of our county. Two of the main sources for our local history – Peadar Livingstone, *The Fermanagh Story*,[1] and William Trimble, *History of Enniskillen*[2] – make minimum reference to organised labour beyond the Land and Labour Leagues which in common with the rest of Ireland. sprang up around the county during the land agitation of the 1880s/1890s. I tried to redress that imbalance in my first effort at writing about the history of the Fermanagh labour movement in 1989 in my Ruskin College thesis, *Labouring on the Margins – A study of The Fermanagh Labour Movement between 1917 and 1923*. An article drawn from this research was published in *Saothar 15*, Journal of the Irish Labour History Society, in 1990.[3]

This publication, to mark the Centenary of Fermanagh Council of Trades Unions, traces a history of workers combining from 1826. It combines an amended version of *Labouring on the Margins* with a piece about Labour's fight for housing in Enniskillen published by Umiskin Press in 2018.[4] This brings the study of Fermanagh labour history up to 1932. In the coming years, it is planned to publish a further history up to the present day.

Fermanagh Trades Council banner on parade, 1980s

# 1

# Fermanagh: A Social, Political & Economic Introduction

County Fermanagh is a rural county of some 700 square miles, situated in the north west of Ireland. It has been part of the Northern Ireland State since Partition in 1921. The mainstay of Fermanagh's economy has been agriculture and fishing and, in more recent times, tourism. The 1926 Census showed that 67.7% of the working population were engaged in agriculture and fishing. Personal services and manufacturing, including building, accounted for only 9% and 7.5% respectively.[5] Fishing in land-locked Fermanagh was based on Lough Erne. The lough stretches the entire length of the county from Belleek in the north to Belturbet in the south. It effectively divides the county in half and floods considerable areas in the winter months.

Due to the predominance of mountain and bog land, agriculture was largely subsistence farming until recent years. In common with many parts of Ireland, Fermanagh did not suffer large-scale emigration from 1911 until 1922. Figures for 1911 show that the total number of emigrants was 443 out of a population of 61,836, less than 1% of the population. This figure declined to just seven by 1918, reflecting the downward trend in national emigration. Emigration did not increase substantially again until the onset of depression in 1921.[6] The reduction in emigration by 1918 can be attributed to a number of factors. Firstly, the economic boom coupled with the reduction in the overall labour force by 9% meant that more jobs were available, thus reducing the need for economic emigration. Secondly, the labour force declined through military recruitment and employment in British munitions factories. A final factor was the danger presented to shipping by wartime conditions, which made it hazardous to travel in the Atlantic or Irish Sea.

For what became a border county, Fermanagh did not suffer much disruption in comparison to other areas of Ireland during the War of Independence or the sectarian strife of 1920. This may be explained because, firstly, while the county's population had a small majority of Catholics, who would have been expected to be Nationalist, the majority was not an overwhelming one. In 1911, Catholics represented 56.18% of the population as compared to just over 43% for other denominations.[7] Secondly, Fermanagh's distance from the main centres of population in Dublin and Belfast, one hundred and ninety miles away respectively, isolated and insulated its rural community from national political trends,

3

at least in the short term. Finally, the predominance of Conservative, Unionist and Nationalist parties in the county tended to preserve the status quo prior to the rise of Sinn Féin. That is not to say that no republican activity took place. There were sporadic incidents which were mainly confined to border villages and on a smaller scale than other areas. This fits in generally with the picture in Ulster, where republican bodies were at their weakest at this time.[8] Sinn Féin did organise in Fermanagh and by October 1921 was reported to have twenty-six clubs in the county[9] Sinn Féin's estimated membership in Fermanagh was 365 per 10,000 of the population by 1919.[10] Total membership, therefore, would have been approximately 2,000 or about 3% of the population. These figures must, however, be qualified because at that time, Sinn Féin clubs also provided an outlet for music, dancing and cultural activities. The number of politically active members may, therefore, have been significantly less than 2,000. In any event, there is no evidence of any significant public political activity by Sinn Féin until the June 1920 County Council election. In this election, Sinn Féin eclipsed the old Nationalists and took control of the County Council. Eventually the Council was suspended for recognising and pledging allegiance to Dáil Éireann.[11]

Enniskillen, the county town, developed on and adjacent to islands between Upper and Lower Lough Erne, has been a major settlement in the west of Ulster since the seventeenth century. Like many other Irish towns, it owes its name to a legend. The town supposedly takes its name from Ceithleann, wife of Balor, the legendary Formorian hero, who found her last resting-place there after the second battle of Moytura. The Irish form of the name is Inis Ceithleann, meaning Island of Kathleen. Enniskillen, with its strategic and defensive advantages, first entered recorded history as a fortress of the Maguire clan in the fifteenth century. It has been a garrison town since the Napoleonic Wars, a factor perhaps in its political conservatism, given that the garrison would have created employment for the townspeople who may have developed an affinity with the military over the years.

According to the 1911 Census, Enniskillen had a population of 4,847. This had increased slightly by 1926 to 4,863. The town had very little industry beyond a co-operative mill and the railway. Employment was largely in services such as carting, tailoring, printing, building and fishing. The town's religious make up was evenly balanced, as indicated by the make-up of the Urban Council immediately after the 1920 Enniskillen Urban Council Elections: 10 Unionists and 11 anti-Unionists.[12] Sectarianism was not openly evident on the Council until after 1920. This mirrors the trend in what was to become Northern Ireland, which was virtually free of open sectarian strife from the First World War until 1920 when the escalation of the war between the Irish Republican Army (IRA) and the British Army began to manifest itself. By the summer of 1920, the economic boom was collapsing. On 20 July the first Catholics were expelled from Belfast's shipyards, soon to be followed by Protestants with labour sympathies.[13]

# 2

# Trade Unions In Fermanagh

The first evidence of combination in Fermanagh was a report in the *Enniskillen Chronicle & Erne Packet* on 23 March 1826.[14] It was an advert notifying the public that local masons and bricklayers had given notice that their hours forthwith were from 6am to 6pm with breaks of one and a half hours per day [a sixty-three hour week based on six days]. The notice suggests that skilled artisans were organised in craft societies before this period in Fermanagh as it refers to applying previous customs

The next significant period is recorded in June 1834. During this period local bakers and tailors were being organised in trade unions to the dismay of the local establishment. Threats were made in the local press to give their names to the judiciary and have them deported to Australia for allegedly being involved in an illegal combination.[15]

This was the fate that had befallen the Tolpuddle Martyrs, a group of Dorset farm labourers led by George Loveless. Loveless, his brother James, James Hammett, James Brine, Thomas Standfield and Thomas's son John were charged with having taken an illegal oath. But their real crime in the eyes of the establishment was to have formed a trade union to protest about their meagre pay of six shillings a week – the equivalent of 30p in today's money and the third wage cut in as many years. After the sentence was pronounced, the working class rose up in support of the Martyrs. A massive demonstration marched through London and an 800,000-strong petition was delivered to Parliament protesting about their sentence. After three years, during which the trade union movement sustained the Martyrs' families by collecting voluntary donations, the Government retreated and the men returned home with free pardons and as heroes. While there is no evidence that the Enniskillen Bakers suffered a similar fate, union organisation would not have been welcomed by the establishment. Irish workers organised protests in support of the Tolpuddle victims and travelled to participate in demonstrations in England.[16] Years later, workers continued to be jailed for standing up for their rights. Local bakers were still organised in the Bakers' Union in 1876.[17]

May 1844 saw workers on the Erne Improvement Works take strike action. There is no mention of whether these workers were in a trade union but they obviously knew the benefit of combining. The dispute concerned the workers being paid fortnightly, having to work compulsory day and night shifts and the coarse language being used by gangers. In the event, the dispute was quickly resolved and the men returned to work.[18]

Two years later in 1846, the local paper reported that labourers employed in the Ely estate outside Enniskillen had gone on strike for an advance in pay. The newspaper was very critical of the strikers and described the Marquis of Ely – who was absent in England – as a very good employer. Presumably if he had been that good the workers would not have needed to strike. It is not clear from the press reports how the dispute ended but it appears strike breakers were used at some stage. The same edition of the paper had a letter from an anonymous apprentice looking for employers to change the hours of closing in their shops to benefit the health of apprentices.[19] These actions are all the more remarkable when it is considered that they took place against a backdrop of the Great Hunger (An Ghorta Mhór) with the population of the county reducing by more than 40,000 between 1841 and 1851.[20]

In, 1854 the Amalgamated Society of Tailors and Tailoresses (ASTT) set up a branch in Fermanagh.[21] The ASTT began life as the Amalgamated Society of Journeymen Tailors, later absorbing other tailors' societies to become the ASTT. By the 1890s, it boasted twenty-seven branches all over Ireland including Enniskillen. The ASTT were stalwart members of the Irish Trades Union Congress (ITUC) and Derryman, James McCarron served as ITUC President on three occasions between 1899 and 1910.[22] McCarron was drowned when a passenger on the *RMS Leinster* when it was sunk by a German U Boat on 10 October 1918.[23]

In May 1856 a meeting of the building trades met in Enniskillen Town Hall. The newspaper report says that the purpose of the meeting was to regulate hours and the attendance was enormous. The meeting was chaired by James Leonard and also in attendance were T. McCormick and John McBrien. The introduction to the meeting is interesting in that they state, 'We do so meet by warrant of a statute of Edward the Seventh, Chapter the Fifth, which empowers tradesmen to meet for the regulation of their trade. We meet legally and not as persons acting contrary to the law'. Part of the meeting gave a report on an employer, Downes, who got men to work overtime but did not pay them the extra. The following resolution was put and carried by the meeting. (Note: There is a report of a similar meeting thirty years before earlier in this publication)

> 'Hours Sought – 6am – 6pm
>
> To work the above with three quarters of an hour for breakfast and 1 hour for dinner.
>
> The necessity for relaxation to be spent in the company of one's family
>
> Maintenance of good health.'[24]

On 24 December 1864, the *Nation* newspaper reported on a meeting of the United Trades Association. The Secretary 'read a communication from Wexford on the subject of the union of trades, the writer, Mr B Hughes, warmly eulogised the movement, and promised his hearty co-operation to a movement having for its object the promotion of a general union of tradesmen and the encouragement of home manufacture. Similar communications from Enniskillen and other towns were read, all in favour of the movement and thanking the committee for their endeavour to cement the trades in their respective localities.' [25]

Although it may not be accepted by our city comrades, in light of this report it could be argued that Enniskillen and other provincial towns were the first ones to develop Trades Councils all those years ago in 1864 long before the founding of either Belfast (1881) or Dublin (1886) Trades Councils or indeed the British Trades Union Congress (1868) or ITUC (1894).

In 1865, workers were still struggling for their rights and local tailors found themselves in dispute with William Carson, a master tailor based in Enniskillen. Carson refused to recognise the union and pay the nationally agreed rates of pay. As a result, his tailors struck work. Carson hired a number of tailors from Dublin to try and break the strike. He engaged them at £1 and 1 shilling per week, paid their expenses and gave them each five shillings. He had not told them that he was in dispute with the Tailors' Union. When they arrived in town, they were advised of the dispute by local tailors who gave them ten shillings and escorted them to the town boundary. Carson took proceedings against both the Dublin Tailors, for breach of contract, and the local tailors for alleged intimidation. In the event a number of local tailors, James Connor, James Magee and Michael Griffin were jailed for a month with hard labour for intimidation, albeit on very flimsy evidence. No appeal or bail was allowed, an indication of the flavour of the justice working people could then expect.[26]

In March 1880, the local paper described conditions as having reached the stage of famine and told its readers of a 'mob' besieging Mr Whitely, Chairman of the Town Commissioners, at the Diamond and causing him considerable annoyance with the cry of 'Work or Bread'. At the same time, men in the local Spool Mill were on strike, so perhaps it was they who were shouting at Whiteley. [27]

In 1888, there was a strike in the Belleek potteries. After five workers were initially dismissed, it descended into rivalries between managers and directors. Matters were resolved in July 1888 and normal work resumed.[28] In 1890, the Enniskillen tailors were involved in a dispute with Master Tailor Quinn based at the Diamond. As in 1865, a number of tailors were taken to court for alleged assaults during the dispute. Interestingly, a John Connor appeared as a witness for the workers and is cited as the local Branch President of the Amalgamated Society of Tailors of Manchester. It may have been him or a relative who was jailed during the 1865 dispute. Connor testified that the men who were on strike were being paid fifteen shillings per week during the strike and that it was the strike breaker who had started the row in a local bar. Unsurprisingly, the strike breaker was not prosecuted. Edward Gallagher was jailed for one month with hard labour on six counts, Monahan was jailed for one month with hard labour and Roper jailed for seven days.[29]

After 1890, evidence of trades union activity is sparse outside of the Land and Labour Leagues which had sprung up in the county in the early 1900s. There is a report of a Land & Labour League meeting in the grounds of Lisnaskea Workhouse where a speaker recommended that the Council workers get themselves organised in a Labour Union to assert their rights.[30] There is no evidence that they did organise, however, although they did so later in the century.

In Lisnaskea, an independent socialist, Thomas Plunkett, challenged the establishment in both Lisnaskea Poor Law Guardians and Lisnaskea Rural Council as an elected member. Plunkett was from the townland of Derryad. It is likely that his activism sprang out of the Land League agitation. According to the 1911 Census, he was a member of the Unitarian Church and lived at Derryad with his wife, sister, three daughters and one son.[31] His views and activities were enough to get him noticed in both Nationalist and Unionist newspapers. A headline in the *Impartial Reporter* in September 1906 stated 'Socialism not well received'.[32]

Lisnaskea Workhouse
*Courtesy of Benny Cassidy and Old Enniskillen Facebook Page*

In December 1907, Plunkett represented tenants from the Manorwater Estate in at a meeting with John C.W. Madden under the Land Act with a view to arriving at terms for a sale. The meeting was a lively one and broke up without agreement being reached. Madden's agent, William Turner, circulated the letter below to tenants after the meeting. Clearly Plunkett's approach or his socialist credentials were not welcomed by the landlord class. Plunkett sent the letter the *Fermanagh Herald*. It demonstrates how landlords tried to intimidate their tenants. The landlord did not, of course, find himself in court like the Tailors mentioned earlier who were accused of intimidation. The letter is as follows,[33]

> 'Men,
>
> In consequence of your selection of Thomas Plunkett, of Derryad, as chairman of the meeting, held on December 30th last – a man who is only a small tenant paying me £5 15s a year, but who is, I learn well known for his socialistic views and therefore no doubt selected by you for this reason, and also in consequence of the speeches there made and the violent behaviour of you all to me (with the exception of Mr John Moore of Moorlaugh and Mr J.J. Russell of Carrarrooskey), I beg to announce to you that I cannot any longer allow you the privilege of coming into my agent's office and paying your rent at any time suitable to yourselves within reasonable limits. I have therefore, determined to establish rent days for my Manorwater property on May 10th and November 10th, or as soon as may be convenient on which my agent will be prepared to receive your rents and of which due notice of time and place will be given. The names of all tenants who do not then pay their rent will be handed the next day to my solicitor in order that proceedings may be at once instituted for their recovery. I regret having to take these steps, but as my Manorwater tenants are evidently exceptionally mean and grasping, and as you choose to adopt the views of a Socialist like Thomas Plunkett, I feel that the only possible relations which can be allowed to exist between us in the future are those of strict business. – John C.W. Madden.'

Clearly Plunkett had irked his landlord. Madden controlled more than 10,500 acres of land in Fermanagh and Monaghan on behalf of his family and was responsible for its sale to tenants under the terms of the Land Act.

In 1907, Jim Larkin's arrival in Belfast on behalf of the Liverpool-based National Union of Dock Labourers culminated in the Dockers' & Carters' Strike. Marked by repressive violence and the deaths of Margaret Lennon and Charles Mullan, unrest and dissatisfaction led the police to go on strike led by Royal Irish Constabulary (RIC) Constable, William Barrett, who had refused to sit beside the blackleg driver of a traction engine being used to break the dockers' strike. The *Impartial Reporter* reported that the Fermanagh RIC gave support to their police colleagues on strike in Belfast with the following telegrams being sent, 'Bravo Barrett – Conference Held – Support certain – money and men. No surrender with a vengeance – Lisnaskea'.[34]

While there is no evidence of other strikes in this period, both Teachers and Shop Assistants were active in the fight for improved conditions of work. The Irish National Teachers' Organisation (INTO) had organised in Fermanagh since at least 1904 when a report of one of their meetings was carried in the *Fermanagh Herald*.[35] Press reports show active branches in Lisnaskea, Irvinestown and Enniskillen. In July 1907, the Enniskillen National Teachers' Association met in the Central Café under the Presidency of Mr Sweeney. The meeting adopted a resolution calling upon the Government to acknowledge the immediate necessity of providing more adequate financial treatment for Irish education and Irish teachers. To that end, they called for a supplementary estimate before that session of Parliament closed.[36] Teachers met again in the Central Café, Enniskillen on 18 January 1908, those present including a Miss Reihill and Messrs Whiteside, Sweeney, Egerton, Keenan, Devaney, Corrigan, Brogan, Curran and Kerrin. The meeting nominated a number of people for the Central Executive in Dublin including Misses Mahon and Larmour.[37] This is one of the few references found to women activists locally beyond a reference to their attendance at a public meeting and their involvement in the Lisbellaw Woollen Factory dispute.

1908 witnessed agitation begin around a half holiday for shop assistants. Under the Shops Act if two thirds of employers could be persuaded the Urban Council could compel all shops to give the half-holiday each week. At the time, many shop assistants worked from 8am to 8pm, six days a week. A delegation representing assistants in drapery, ironmongers, grocers and boot and shoe shops met the employers. Shop assistants in Omagh had won the concession the previous summer.[38]

Saddlers also made a request for their half-holiday to be on a Saturday to suit the conditions of their trade.[39] The Urban Council agreed to begin implementation of the Shop Hours Act with only one Councillor dissenting, Councillor Cooper because the grocery shop owners were opposed to it.[40] The half day was approved by the Lord Lieutenant in October 1908.[41] The closing order was posted by the Council on 17 October 1908.[42] It is not clear if any trade union was involved but there was an Enniskillen Branch of the Irish Drapers' Assistants' Association (IDAA) in existence in 1912 when the press reported a party of forty from the local branch having an excursion to the Marble Arches.[43] Taking the shop assistants' lead, Urban Council workers also applied for a half day holiday. In the event Enniskillen Urban Council refused a half day holiday to their workers.[44]

Local newspapers carried no further reports of union activity between 1912 and the beginning of the First World war on 28 July 1914. This is perhaps unsurprising given the Home Rule agitation and the onset of war. After 1916 and the Easter Rising, Irish trade union membership increased dramatically with unions catering for the unskilled experiencing the largest increases. The Irish Transport & General Workers Union (ITGWU), for example, had ten branches and 5,000 members in 1916. By the end of 1918, it had 210 branches and 67,287 members.[45] Industrial unions like the National Union of Railwaymen (NUR) experienced similar, rapid growth. In 1916, the NUR only organised one in six of Irish railway workers. By 1920, it had 20,000 members and 120 branches.[46]

This upsurge in union membership came partly from the wartime economy. A boom in agriculture and other areas of the economy, which lasted until the early 1920s, boosted employment and workers' bargaining power. The war occasioned dependence on native producers. It was estimated that by 1917, 90% of the domestic beef market was supplied by British and Irish farmers as opposed to 60% in 1914.[47] Irish farmers were doing well out of the war. Unskilled workers, however, were not doing so well. By 1917, the cost of living index had risen 125% above pre-war levels with no corresponding rise in wages.[48] This ensured support for any organisation which offered workers a chance to improve their real wages. Other factors contributing to union growth were the radicalisation of the country after the Rising and the fact that the available labour force had shrunk by 9% thus enhancing workers bargaining power.

These favourable social and economic conditions allowed unions to expand their memberships. While the ITGWU were successful in a line south of Dundalk to Sligo, in Ulster they did not penetrate very deeply, mainly because their known Nationalist sympathies alienated Protestant workers. In the North therefore, British-based Unions held sway.[49] The Fermanagh Labour movement in 1917 was characterised by the absence of unions for the unskilled. Trade unions were either of the craft or industrial variety. Those operating at that time were the NUR, INTO, Typographical Association (TA), Postal Telegraph Society, Postmen's Federation, Manchester Unity Operative Bricklayers, House & Ship Painters Association (Manchester), IDAA, ASTT and the Amalgamated Society of Woodworkers (ASW). Of the ten, only the IDAA and INTO were Irish-based. The remainder were British-based. The range of unions indicates available employment outside agriculture.

There is very little evidence of these trade unions' activity during the war years, with a few exceptions. For example, the INTO Branch was successful in April 1917 in getting a motion passed by Fermanagh County Council calling for a portion of the £6 million granted to education in Britain, to be shared with Ireland.[50] It was part of a national campaign by teachers to pressurise the British Government to increase funding for Irish education.[51]

In June 1917, the Enniskillen NUR Branch held a meeting in the Town Hall under the chairmanship of a George Newell. The meeting was addressed by NUR Irish Secretary Nathan Rimmer. It called upon all railway workers to join the union and for the Executive to resolve the question of war bonus for 'shop-men'.[52] This refers to the seven shillings bonus paid to Irish railway workers after a threatened strike in 1916. Unlike their British counterparts,

Irish railwaymen did not receive the normal War Bonus because Irish railways were not taken over by the Government at the outbreak of war. The only other report during the war, was a reference in the local nationalist paper, the *Fermanagh Herald,* to a dance, organised by the IDAA, being disrupted by British soldiers, who tore down decorations. This may have been in line with attacks being made on unions with nationalist sentiments after the Easter Rising. The ITGWU had suffered very badly during this period from raids on offices and the arrest of officials. The IDAA was Dublin-based. As the military authorities apologised for the incident, it may not have been sanctioned by them.[53]

In common with other trade unions in the north of Ireland during the war, Fermanagh unions do not appear to have been particularly active or militant. This is borne out to some degree by strike statistics for the period. They were no recorded disputes between 1914-1918.[54] These statistics though must be qualified because they do not include political strikes or those involving less than ten people or lasting less than one day. It can, however, be assumed that strike action was at a minimum, given the predominance of British-based unions. Both Irish and British based unions would have been governed by war time Defence of the Realm Act (DORA) regulations preventing them from causing industrial disruption.

# 3

# *Organising the Labourers:*
# *The National Amalgamated Union*
# *of Labour*

The Fermanagh labour movement was about to be enlivened by the organisation of the unskilled workers. On 2 January 1918, a meeting was held in Enniskillen Town Hall, addressed by a Dublin union organiser called E.P. Harte and two local men – Michael McCarney, a National Union of Railwaymen (NUR) member, and William Clarke (Postmen's Federation. PF). Harte went on to become the Irish Secretary of the ATGWU, 1922-1924. It was decided to set up an organising committee and hold a public meeting a week later, to launch a branch of the National Amalgamated Union of Labour (NAUL).[55] Until 1893, the NAUL was known as the Tyneside & National Labour Union and began as an organisation for the semi-skilled and unskilled workers in the shipyards of North East England. It spread rapidly to other local industries and by 1893 had established itself in Ireland, with a base in Belfast, although 19,000 of its 23,000 members were still based in the North East of England.[56] The NAUL was originally led by 'Lib-Labs' but after the election of A. T. Dipper as General Secretary in 1893, it adopted a socialist position.

The influence of the NAUL's Irish membership is best demonstrated by the fact that George Grieg, later to be the Irish Official Delegate, was elected NAUL President in 1901. The NAUL grew dramatically from 1910, when it had 16,000 members, to 1920 when it had 143,000 members.[57] According to the union's 1918 *Quarterly and Annual Report*, membership in the Belfast district, (later re-named Irish District) increased from 7,041 members in thirteen branches at March 1917 to 12,762 in twenty-seven branches by June 1918. The name change to Irish District reflected the increased membership outside Belfast.[58]

NAUL reports branches were widespread across Ulster from Portadown in the east to Letterkenny in the west, organising those as diverse as local authority workers in Armagh to farm servants in Donegal. The NAUL now began to organise in Fermanagh. Its inaugural meeting was chaired by J.P. Gillen, Nationalist Chairman of the Urban Council and a man of apparently liberal views. He welcomed the NAUL's formation so that all might get a decent wage. Also present at the meeting, which according to local press reports was well attended, was George Grieg, Irish Delegate. Grieg outlined the benefits of membership, while stressing that the NAUL was not a revolutionary organisation. This was undoubtedly a reference to the Irish Transport & General Workers' Union (ITGWU), who were often categorised as 'Bolshevik' or 'Sinn Féin' or both!. William Clarke and Sam Bradley, a NAUL official from Belfast, also addressed the gathering. Bradley provided some idea of the unskilled workers' lot. He told the meeting that labourers' wages in Enniskillen ranged from 18s to £1 per week on average. Out of this, rent at 4s 6d, coal at 6s 6d and milk at 3s 6d had to be taken, leaving the sum of 3s 6d for all the other necessities of life.[59] This was a common picture at the time. For example, when the Agricultural Wages Board was established in September 1917, it set agricultural wages at 25s for County Dublin and 20s for the rest of the country.[60] This was at a time when the cost of living had risen 120% by 1918. Unskilled workers increasingly saw the union as the only way out of poverty.

Wages were not, however, to be the first major issue which the NAUL found itself involved with in Fermanagh. In 1918. the British Government announced plans to introduce Conscription in Ireland. The announcement met with opposition from all shades of Nationalist opinion and Labour. Nationally, Labour responded by calling an extra-ordinary Conference on 20 April,1918. Attended by 1,500 delegates, it decided to call a twenty-four hour strike from midnight on 23 April. The purpose of the strike was to act as

Middleton Street,
site of first NAUL office

'A demonstration of fealty to the cause of Labour and Ireland, a sign of resolve to resist the Conscription Act, and finally, to enable every man and woman to sign the pledge of resistance.'[61]

The strike was a resounding success outside of Belfast and led to the British Government abandoning their plans for Conscription. In Fermanagh, while there was reference to the strike in the local press, no actual strike action took place. The Labour movement in the county did, nonetheless, express its opposition to Conscription in two ways. Firstly, the Enniskillen NAUL branch passed a motion condemning Conscription and the continuance of what they described as a 'Capitalist War'.[62] The motion was sent to the leaders of the main political parties in Ireland and the NAUL General Secretary.

The second contribution came from William Clarke, by now the local NAUL spokesman. Clarke was born in Westmeath in 1883. In 1911, he was working as a Postman in Enniskillen and lived at 3 Mill Street with his mother and three siblings. The family were Church of Ireland.[63] Clarke addressed a large anti-Conscription rally in Enniskillen, attended by various shades of Nationalist opinion and Catholic clergy. In his address, Clarke said, 'I know the feelings of both Protestant and Catholic workers and none of them favour Conscription being forced upon them'. While pledging Labour's opposition to Conscription, Clarke also took the opportunity to condemn the unfair treatment and low pay of Irish workers.[64]

The difference in approach by Labour in Fermanagh to this issue as compared to Dublin and Belfast is worth noting. In Dublin and the south generally, Labour was unequivocal in its opposition to Conscription. Belfast on the other hand, with a few exceptions, did not support the campaign against Conscription because of its Unionist majority. Fermanagh, while it had a Nationalist majority, also had a substantial Unionist population. This presented Labour with a dilemma. To ignore the anti-Conscription campaign would alienate Nationalists, but too much action might alienate Unionists. Hence, the strategy of stopping short of strike action in an attempt to appease both sides. In the event, alienation did take place and was to lead to the NAUL losing some Protestant members.[65]

With Conscription abandoned, the NAUL proceeded to tackle low pay in the county. In August 1918, an application from the NAUL was submitted to Enniskillen Urban Council for a rise in wages to 30s (from 22s 6d) a week for labourers. In response, the Urban Council agreed to pay an increase of 3s 6d, bringing street cleaners rates up to 26s a week. This wage agitation was not taking place in isolation. Evidence of increased agitation can be seen from strike statistics for the period which showed that strikes increased dramatically in Ireland from just after the war until 1921. These strikes showed a different pattern from previously, spreading from urban areas into the countryside, and from the traditionally militant areas of building, metal and textiles, to normally docile areas of employment.[66] This trend was also experienced in Fermanagh, where recorded strikes increased from nil during the war years, to three in the old sector of building, metal and textiles, and four in the new sectors, between the end of the war and 1921.

The NAUL campaigned for increased wages, for both Urban and County Council workers. This led to a claim from both groups for 35s a week in the autumn of 1918. Both Councils conceded the claim after a threat of industrial action. The NAUL did not confine their activities to local councils, successfully challenging private employers and obtaining 35s a week for labourers after a short strike. Likewise, they did not restrict their activities to the bigger employers. For example, they made representations on behalf of one member sacked for claiming a pay rise while employed by Derrygonnelly Co-operative, a small village co-operative ten miles from

Enniskillen. They also crossed swords with the local Poor Law Guardians, over the wages of a ferryman and ambulance-man, who were paid 21s for a seven-day week. If the ITGWU were trying to organise the labourers of Ireland, in Fermanagh the NAUL were doing a similar job.

The reaction of the local establishment to the NAUL's activities is best summed up by the observations from two employers. One Poor Law Guardian described their activities as 'Kaiserism' and a second, Mr Archdale, a prominent landowner and County Councillor said 'this labour union is going to destroy the labourers of Ireland as it is upsetting them and putting them out of work'.[67] James Bradley, a future Labour Councillor, took him to task at an election hustings in the Butter Market in December 1918 questioning his position on both unions and women's suffrage.[68] Whatever Archdale thought, one thing is certain, the agitation was widespread. Wage movements were being reported throughout the north-west in Derry, Omagh and Enniskillen. Such was the pressure on the NAUL that they had to appoint two additional officials in the north-west alone during 1918.[69]

According to NAUL reports, by early autumn 1918 the Enniskillen Branch had 181 members. By November, when the union launched its campaign to recruit agricultural labourers, an advertisement in the *Fermanagh Times* claimed 400 members, with branches in Blacklion, Derrygonnelly, Irvinestown, Lisbellaw and Florencecourt.[70] This NAUL campaign to recruit agricultural labourers is significant because elsewhere a similar campaign had been initiated by the ITGWU. This organisation of rural labourers by an urban-based union had no precedent in Ireland. It was undertaken because the leaders of the ITGWU wanted to develop One Big Union in Ireland, which catered for all workers.[71] They had also recognised the need to widen their base beyond Dublin after the near collapse of the union in the wake of the 1913 Dublin Lockout. After 1917, much of the expansion was spontaneous and organic, the union surfing the wave rather than stirring the water. That said, this expansion into rural areas like Fermanagh was new.

In organising Irish workers, agricultural labourers could not be ignored as they represented a quarter of the total workforce and half the manual workforce.[72] Of equal importance was the fact that poor wages, conditions and shortage of continuous work drove rural labour into the towns looking for work. This threatened the position of urban union members by creating greater competition for employment, thus driving wage rates down. Problems were, however, to be encountered in the organisation of rural workers. Prior to the First World War, agricultural labourers had adopted a subservient attitude, tending to be thankful to paternalistic employers for providing jobs and asking little in return. Many labourers hungered for land rather than monetary gain. This hunger was whetted to some degree by a Government Scheme which gave labourers an acre plot of land to work for themselves. A further factor, which increased hunger for land, was the

Nationalist ideology which portrayed the labourer as an evicted tenant who would someday repossess the land stolen from his ancestors.

These problems were overcome by war-time economic conditions which increased the importance of the agricultural labourer, as farmers switched to labour-intensive tillage to meet wartime needs. Conditions of economic boom raised the labourer's expectations without satisfying their economic needs. As farmers prospered, labourers became discontent with poor wages and turned to trade unionism. Labourers sensed an enhanced bargaining position and gains were therefore achieved relatively easily. It was in such an environment that the NAUL began organising Fermanagh's agricultural workers in the winter of 1918. The ITGWU had endeavoured to organise agricultural workers in Lisnaskea and Newtownbutler, probably under the leadership of Peadar O'Donnell. The ITGWU two branches, 185 at Lisnaskea where Francis McCormick of Whitepark was Branch Secretary and another 202 at Newtownbutler where Owen Reilly of Gortgormon was Secretary.[73] The NAUL in Fermanagh had some local advantage as they claimed considerable success in improving labourers' wages in the urban area over the preceding year.

The NAUL campaign began with a public meeting organised in Paget Square, Enniskillen, chaired by J. Bradley. Motions were put to the meeting by John Campbell, a labour activist and elected Councillor in Belfast's Dock Ward. Also attending were Doherty (Derry, NAUL) and William Logue, Chairman, Derry Trades Council. The meeting passed resolutions calling for the enforcement of compulsory tillage regulations, the ending of the hiring system, an increase in the cultivation of potatoes, the publication of Agricultural Wages Board Minutes and, finally, a pledge to deal only with unionised employers.[74] All these demands were directly relevant to the agricultural labourer in that their implementation would provide more jobs, cheaper food, an end to the exploitation of the hiring system, and, more control over the rates set by the Wages Board. So began the campaign in Fermanagh and it was soon apparent that both unions were having some impact.

A number of agricultural strikes were recorded in 1919. They started in February with a small farm strike. This was followed in March with a strike in Lisnaskea where blackleg labour was used to break the strike. One striker, Coyle, was prosecuted for abusing a blackleg. In April a dispute took place in Newtownbutler during which three tons of hay were burnt.[75] An indication of NAUL success was the fact that in February 1919 farmers began to organise in the Farmers' Union (FU), while at the time they claimed not to be combining against the workmen. This has to be doubted in light of the fact that in March 1919 the Lisnaskea FU Branch announced plans to form a 'Labour Corps' to break strikes where labourers refused to accept Wage Board rates – rates regarded by farmers as a maximum rather than a minimum.[76] In April 1919 Enniskillen farmers took a similar decision. Quite clearly, a concerted attempt was being made to break rural

Paget Square
*Courtesy Benny Cassidy and Old Enniskillen FacebookPage*

trade union organisation. The remainder of 1919 saw very little further NAUL activity on this front, beyond a call at the 1920 May Day Rally in Enniskillen by William Clarke for farm labourers to join the union.[77] By 1923 there is no record of the two ITGWU branches in Lisnaskea and Newtownbutler but the NAUL were still in existence. This was not unusual as small rural branches often declined and recreated themselves several times over a period of years.

In Fermanagh, and throughout Ireland, recruitment of farm workers declined from 1920. The decline set in as the agricultural boom collapsed and unemployment increased when the policy of compulsory tillage ended. This coupled with the dismantling of minimum wage protection, led to a position where unions could only hope to defend what they had, rather than gain increases. The situation in Fermanagh mirrored that elsewhere and little further mention is made of organising farm workers during this period. Nonetheless, the struggles of the NAUL to organise the unskilled do not seem to have gone unnoticed by other unions. Their example led to several organising drives by others. For example, the National Union of Life Assurance Workers held a meeting locally in October 1918 and successfully recruited a number of members including one woman. Another example was that of the Vintners' Assistants' Association who concluded an agreement on opening hours with Enniskillen Vintners in March 1919.[78] The major lessons learnt by the struggles of the urban and agricultural labourers by other unions, was the need for unity between craft, industrial and general workers. That realisation was to lead to the formation of Enniskillen Trades and Labour Council in 1919.

# 4

# *Spade and Trade Unite: The Founding of Enniskillen Trades and Labour Council 1919*

1919 opened to find the National Amalgamated Union of Labour (NAUL) and the Enniskillen Poor Law Guardians locked in a dispute over the wages of the ambulance-man and ferryman. The NAUL Executive had made the dispute official in November 1918.[79] In the event, the solidarity shown by local gas-workers, who refused to handle coke supplies for the workhouse, led to the Guardians conceding a rise to 31s, just 4s less than that demanded. This was 10s a week more than Cleary, the ambulance-man, had been receiving a few months earlier for a 70-hour week. The unskilled workers had shown that their support for each other could bring even the hardest employer to the negotiating table.

This example of strength through unity was the background to the founding of Enniskillen Trades & Labour Council (ET&LC), which combined local unions in fighting for the broader social and economic issues facing the working class. On the 21 February 1919, the ET&LC was formed at a meeting in Enniskillen Town Hall under the auspices of the NAUL. The meeting was presided over by William Clarke, who had by then been appointed as a part-time NAUL Assistant Irish Official Delegate.[80] The object of the meeting was to form a trades council in Enniskillen, where each trade society would be represented by two delegates. In attendance at the meeting were Thomas Cassidy, Irish Organiser, Typographical Association (TA) and President of the Irish Labour Party & Trade Union Congress; John Farnham, Chairman, Omagh Trades Council; and William Logue, Chairman, Derry Trades Council.

The resolution to form a provisional council was moved by a Mr Brennan, Secretary of the Irish Drapers' Assistants' Association (IDAA) and seconded by J. Fox, Secretary of the Amalgamated Union of Co-Operative & Commercial & Allied Workers (AUCCAW).[81] The first provisional Executive Council was T. Sweeney (Irish National Teachers' Organisation (INTO); P. O'Neill (Discharged Soldiers' & Sailors' Federation); M. McCarney (National Union of Railwaymen, NUR); T. Fitzpatrick (IDAA): J. Fox (AUCCAW)); P. J. Keaveny (TA): P. McNulty (Postal Telegraph Society, PTS); William Clarke (Postmen's Federation, PF); C. McKeown (NAUL); T. McManus (National Union of Life Assurance Agents, NULAA); and W.

Kelly (Amalgamated Society of Tailors & Tailoresses, AST&T).[82] These were joined in October 1919 by representatives of the Amalgamated Society of Woodworkers (ASW), Manchester Unity Operative Bricklayers and the House & Ship Painters' Association, Manchester.[83]

Irish trades councils date from the 1860s when the United Trades Association of Dublin called upon trade societies in other Irish towns to come together where three or more societies existed. What were believed to be the oldest trades councils in Ireland were formed in Belfast in 1881 and Dublin in 1886.[84] It was not, however, until the closing years of the First World War, accompanied by the resurgence of union activity, that trades councils began to spring up all over Ireland. For example, in 1916 the number of trades councils attending the ITUC&LP Congress was only five. By the 1919 Congress this had increased to 30 and peaked at 46 by 1921.[85] In the north west, Derry Trades Council is thought to be the oldest continuous council having been formed in 1898. Now however, trades councils were being formed throughout the north west, with Omagh, Strabane, Coleraine and Enniskillen all having councils by the end of 1919. In 1919, Enniskillen is reported as being affiliated with 800 members and William Clarke is listed as the delegate to the 1919 Congress.[86]

Trades councils emerged for a number of reasons. The organisational drive by Congress encouraged the formation of trades councils where enough unions existed. The presence of ILP&TUC President Thomas Cassidy at the initial meeting of the Enniskillen Council supports this contention. Wage agitation and subsequent successes had given workers confidence in their ability to improve, not only wages, but social conditions as well. The absence of open sectarianism in the north and the fact that all-out war with Britain had not yet developed in the south assisted attempts to bring workers together. Finally, at a local level, it seems likely that the local Labour Club played a part in the formation of the Trades Council. The Labour Club had been formed in January 1918 and had a membership of fifty at that time. Its role was to spread trades unionism and Labour ideas in the area.[87]

ET&LC had a greater role in labour movement activities than is the case in modern councils. For example, they not only promoted the social and economic policies of the ILP&TUC, they acted as mediators in local industrial disputes. Their first business meeting was held in March 1919 in the local Irish National Foresters Hall. At that meeting, annual subscriptions were agreed at sixpence a member and the Officers and Executive Committee were elected. Not surprisingly, William Clarke was elected Chairman. Vice-Chairman was J. Fox and the Secretary was P. J. McNulty. Executive Members were W. Kelly, C. Rose, J. Irvine, J. McGovern, T. McManus, S. Boyd and P. Keaveny. With administrative matters settled, the Council got down to discussing the ongoing building dispute, which had begun in early March 1919.[88]

1919 was a period when the building trade experienced a boom. The unions in the trade were quick to seek to improve members' wages and conditions. The National Federation of Building Trade Operatives (NFBTO) were often involved in these disputes. The NFBTO was founded in 1918 and was the most highly developed of the trade federations. It covered unions in building and construction and employed full-time regional officers to look after its affairs. NFBTO had a great deal of authority in regard to strike action and it conducted most of the national wage negotiations for the industry.[89]

The Enniskillen dispute was for an increase in wages and a decrease in hours. The strike lasted about four weeks and the level of support it engendered can be gauged by reports in the local press. A march of several hundred workers took place around Enniskillen in support of the building unions. The march was led by the red NAUL banner, which urged workers to join the union and abolish slavery.[90] The front section of this red banner read

'N.A.U.L.

UNITED WE LIVE – DIVIDED WE STARVE

WORKER, IF YOU ARE NOT IN A UNION

YOU ARE AN ENEMY TO YOURSELF

AND AN ENEMY TO YOUR FAMILY'

The ET&LC, as well as giving support, played the role of mediator when it was reported to their March meeting that one employer wished to settle. A delegation of three – McNulty, McManus and T. Fitzpatrick – were elected to meet the employer. With the co-operation of J.P. Gillin, Chairman of the Urban Council, they secured a settlement. The workers' demands had ranged from 35s a week for labourers, to 50s for tradesmen and a reduction in hours to fifty-one with a half-day on Saturdays. The settlement gave labourers 33s a week, and tradesmen 46s. Hours were reduced to fifty-two and new overtime rates were agreed.[91] The ET&LC undoubtedly enhanced their standing with local workers after securing such a significant settlement.

Local employers were far from pleased, however, and attempted to vent their anger on Stewart Boyd, a member of the ET&LC Executive. Boyd, who was also Town Sergeant, a cross between Doorman and Master of Ceremonies for the Urban Council, was accused of intimidating blacklegs during the dispute by threatening to throw one over the west bridge. In the event, after investigation, he was exonerated by the Urban Council.[92] In 1911, Boyd was a gas labourer living at in Forthill Street, Enniskillen with his wife Annie and two children. The family were Church of Ireland.[93] They later moved to live in Paget Square. Boyd died a few months after his retirement in October 1941.[94]

It is perhaps appropriate to compare this settlement with rates enjoyed by building trade workers in Dublin. The Dublin Building Trade Employers'

Association were paying labourers £3.0.8d for a forty-seven-hour week in late 1919. Dublin Corporation, on the other hand were paying £2.13s a week.[95] Even allowing for the differential between city and countryside, Fermanagh building workers had a lot of ground to make up. ET&LC support for workers in struggle was not just confined to local disputes. In April 1919 they also pledged support for the Omagh branch of the Irish Asylum Workers' Union. These workers were fighting for a 56-hour week and despite threats and intimidation, were eventually successful in their demands.[96]

In April 1919, the EL&TC got involved in the issues of sanitation and housing, with specific reference to the Abbey Street and Dame Street areas located in Enniskillen's predominantly working class North Ward. ET&LC demands were initially rejected by the Urban Council but persistence bore fruit. In July, a new sanitation scheme was initiated at New Row, an area owned by Lord Enniskillen. The scheme was to become the subject of controversy when local unions discovered that those working on the scheme were strike breaking. In the light of this discovery, the unions refused to allow the scheme to progress until the dispute was settled.[97] Local unions were clearly not prepared to accept social improvements at any price. On the housing front, the ET&LC began to make significant progress. A report to the Housing Committee of the Urban Council in June 1919 showed that 200 families in Enniskillen were badly housed. The report emphasised the need for a new housing scheme.[98] The report led to an ET&LC deputation meeting the Urban Council in August to discuss housing and employment. The outcome of the meeting was that ET&LC representatives were allowed onto the Housing Committee as advisers. By October 1919, the ET&LC campaign had resulted in the Urban Council announcing plans to build 350 new homes in Enniskillen.[99] In September 1919, the Housing Department of the Local Government Board had instructed councils to prepare and submit housing schemes. Initial housing schemes were expected to be submitted by November 1919 and at that stage plans for 16,000 houses had been submitted.[100]

On the employment front, agitation by the NAUL and ET&LC led to Fermanagh County Council agreeing, despite opposition, to take advantage of the unemployment relief scheme, in the form of a Road Board Grant. Other areas of ET&LC activity included campaigning for the fair implementation of the Turf Order, to ensure it did not militate against the poor. Equally important, was their campaign to have the provisions of the Profiteering Act implemented locally.[101] Profiteering was a serious problem during and after the War. It was estimated that by 1918, 90 to 95% of beef was being sold above the Government regulated price.[102] In Enniskillen, despite the opposition of some Councillors, the ET&LC succeeded in getting the Urban Council to implement the necessary provisions of the act. In addition, they were invited to nominate three members to the Urban

Council Profiteering Act Committee.[103] In this way the ET&LC was able to make practical use of its influence to control prices locally.

1919 witnessed Fermanagh's first May Day Rally. There was a difference in emphasis shown in Fermanagh as compared to elsewhere in Ireland. In the south, Labour Day was announced as a general holiday so that the working class could join with the international labour movement in demanding a Democratic League of Free Nations, as the necessary condition of permanent peace, based upon self - determination of all peoples, including the Irish people.[104] Fermanagh's approach to Labour Day was somewhat different. Firstly, there is no evidence that a general holiday was taken in the county, although the local NAUL Branch Secretary, John Maguire, did apply to the Urban Council for a half-holiday for his members. In the event, the Council did not discuss his application until after May Day. Nonetheless, a Labour Day march took place. The local press described it as a large procession led by the banners of the NAUL and the Manchester Unity Operative Bricklayers, accompanied by a band. Speeches from Bradley (NAUL) and ET&LC President Clarke emphasised the hypocrisy of politicians and declared no loyalty to any political party but the Labour movement.[105] The question of self-determination was carefully avoided in the speeches. An indication perhaps that Clarke and his colleagues had learnt from the experience of the Anti-Conscription campaign to avoid potentially divisive issues. Their caution did not, however, prevent the Ulster Workers' Trade Union (UWTU) attacking them.

The UWTU was formed in December 1918 to organise the non-unionised Protestant workers in Ulster, who might otherwise have joined the NAUL or the ITGWU. Its leader was James Turkington, who declared in the 1920 Municipal Election campaign that he was 'fighting revolution, bolshevism and rampant socialism'.[106] This was a common tag, which the Unionist Party tried to attach to both Labour and Sinn Féin, in an attempt to portray them as one and the same enemy. Generally, most other unions saw the UWTU as a yellow sectarian union and largely refused to co-operate with it.

A UWTU branch was formed in Fermanagh at a meeting on 13 May 1919 in Enniskillen Orange Hall. The meeting was addressed by Turkington who condemned both Sinn Féin and the ILP&TUC as Bolshevik! He attacked the 1919 May Day stoppage in a similar vein, despite local Labour's avoidance of the National Question. Fermanagh's first UWTU branch had the following officers: Chairman, W. Charlton; Vice Chairman, J. Walker; Secretary, B. Jeffers; and Assistant Secretary, W. Dundas. Dundas was later elected as a Unionist member of Enniskillen Urban Council.[107] Although the UWTU did not cause any serious disruption initially in the local labour movement, their activities in later years would cause division.

In the meantime, while the ET&LC was campaigning on social issues in the county, wage agitation was continuing. In August, the Urban Council agreed to increase carters' wages to £2.0.3s a week, and labourers to £1.17s.6d.

Enniskillen Orange Hall which was also known as the Protestant Hall
(Now known as the Intech Centre)
*Courtesy Pat D'Arcy*

More significantly, agitation was spreading from Enniskillen to the outlying areas. At the end of May 1919, a dispute in Belleek pottery led to the town's electricity supply – which was dependent on the pottery – being cut off. The dispute lasted until late June 1919.[108] In the south of the county, six miles from Enniskillen, a dispute over rates of pay broke out at Lisbellaw Woollen Mills in June. Negotiations had been going on with the employers, Henderson & Eadie, for five months but despite a recommendation from the Ministry of Labour that the dispute go to arbitration, the employer refused to co-operate.[109] The sequel to this dispute was the eviction of a number of workers from their tied houses by Henderson & Eadie. This took place despite the efforts of a local solicitor, Mr. Herbert, who advised the union to take the case to the King`s Bench. Herbert also described the employers as 'sweaters', who were paying a top rate of 12s 6d to girls in their mill. During the hearing one of the owners, Eadie, had said he did not know why the workers had left off working. This was the first dispute in Fermanagh where both women and men went on strike against what was a particularly nasty employer. Even though the employer had, on his own testimony, four or five tied houses laying empty and even though the workers were prepared to pay rent, he insisted on having them evicted. Amongst those evicted were Emily Shaw and her mother, Owen Connolly, John Miller and Mary Mc Mulkin.[110] In a stinging rebuke in the next week's paper, William Logue told readers that the dispute over pay had been going from October 1918 and in February the company had been offered the option of arbitration but would not enter into any discussion. Logue was very critical of the wage rates which he said were '12s 6d per week', poor wages even for those times.[111] This seems to have been a particularly nasty dispute and the NAUL records show that they paid a number of workers removal expenses to enable them to seek employment elsewhere.[112] Interestingly after the Second World War, workers in Lisbellaw Woollen mills rose again under the leadership of the county's veteran trade union leader Jimmy Brown (now deceased) who organised ninety-nine out of a hundred workers in the mill and gained increases of between 4s 6d and 7s 6d per week.[113]

The closing months of 1919 saw carpenters in the employ of James Harvey & Sons, J. Donnelly and H. Pierce on strike for a wage increase and reduced

Lisbellaw Woollen Mill
*Courtesy Benny Cassidy and Old Enniskillen Facebook Page*

hours. They succeeded after a short dispute in having their hours reduced from fifty-two to forty-eight, and their wages increased from £2.10s.0d to £3.4s.0d. per week.[114] This emphasis on reducing hours, as well as increasing wages, may have been due to the partially successful forty-four-hour strike in the Belfast engineering industry in January, which secured a forty-eight hour week. The ILP&TUC had launched an hours and wages campaign in January to encourage such demands and a similar NFBTO strategy resulted in them gaining the eight-hour day and forty-four hour week in 1920.[115] This final factor was probably the most important as the drive for shorter hours seems to have been confined to the Fermanagh building trade. There is no evidence of a similar movement on hours amongst Council workers for example.

The end of 1919 also witnessed the political awakening of Labour in Fermanagh. As already stated, there had been a Labour Club in the county from 1918 and part of its role would have been the promotion of Labour representation. There had been suggestions in October 1918, by way of a letter in the *Fermanagh Times,* that there should be Labour representation on the Urban Council.[116] In November 1918 a Labour candidate was to be put forward in North Fermanagh for the General Election.[117] This was the controversial General Election where George Irvine, a Republican Candidate from a local Protestant family, had to stand down in the face of opposition from the local members of the Ancient Order of Hibernians who would not countenance supporting him because his parents sold tracts and bibles in Enniskillen. There appears to be no evidence of a Labour candidate running for public office until the Local Government elections of 1920.

# 5

# *Labour Representation -*
# *The 1920 Election*

1 920 was a year of contrasts for the Irish Labour movement. In January, Labour gained seats in Councils all over Ireland in an unprecedented show of support. Between May and December, the Munitions Strike almost crippled communications in the country.[118] By July, the battle between Republican and British Government forces was gripping the south-west and in Belfast sectarian violence broke out and was to last two years.[119] How then did Irish Labour respond to this atmosphere in the north and north-west? The Munitions Strike broke out in mid May 1920, when Dublin quayside workers refused to handle war materials. The dispute soon spread to other ports and the railway network. The workers involved undoubtedly saw their actions as similar to, although not in support of, the Hands Off Russia Campaign being conducted by British Workers. The Hands Off Russia campaign was an international political initiative first launched by British socialists in 1919 to organise opposition to British intervention on the side of the White armies in the Russian Civil War. The movement was encouraged by the fledgling Communist International and was ultimately emulated in several other countries, including the United States, Canada and Australia. The expected support from the National Union of Railwaymen (NUR) and British Labour movement for the Irish action was not forthcoming, except in the limited form of supportive resolutions. In Ireland the Irish Labour Party & Trades Union Congress (ILP&TUC) did set up a Munitions of War Fund, which eventually realised £120,000. Generally though, individual unions did not get officially involved in the dispute. By July, nearly a thousand railwaymen had been dismissed and by late November a crisis point was reached with the total closure of the railway system threatened. At a conference in the Mansion House in December railwaymen voted unanimously for a return to work. The Munitions Strike was over. Despite accusations to the contrary, it had not been simply a Republican plot. Rather, it was a spontaneous reaction from Irish workers to the British military presence in Ireland.[120]

Fermanagh experienced some of the effects of the dispute. A well-known guard, Andrew Breslin, was suspended by his company, the Great Northern Railway (GNR). He had refused to work the Enniskillen to Dundalk line when a train was boarded by armed police.[121] He was subsequently dismissed after twenty-seven years' service with the railways. Another guard, Hegarty, was also disciplined for a similar offence on the Enniskillen to Sligo line.[122] In August, further action was reported when a signalman at Newtownbutler refused to let a troop train pass, causing a two-hour delay.[123] By late September, the GNR line between Enniskillen and Dundalk had been closed and closure of the entire system was threatened. This was the last report of local action, beyond a report in early 1922 saying that thirty members were still out of work as a result of the dispute, including a number from Enniskillen.[124]

As was the case in most of Ireland, other unions in Fermanagh appear to have stayed out of the dispute. Indeed, Labour in Fermanagh seems to have avoided any involvement in the main political strikes of the time. The one exception being the Limerick General Strike, which the Enniskillen and Manorhamilton Branch of the Irish National Teachers' Organisation (INTO) made a donation to it.[125] The Limerick Soviet was a self-declared soviet that existed from 15-27 April 1919 in Limerick city. At the beginning of the Irish War of Independence, a general strike was organised by the Limerick Trades & Labour Council, as a protest against the British Army's declaration of a 'Special Military Area' under the Defence of the Realm Act (DORA), which covered most of Limerick City and part of the county. The Soviet ran the city for the period, printed its own money and organised the supply of food amongst other services.

Labour in Fermanagh entered the local political arena at a time when Labour nationally was at the height of its influence and the political situation was very fluid. The Labour Party had stayed out of the 1918 General Election, despite opposition in its ranks, to leave the way open for a clear expression by the Irish people of their wholehearted support for self-determination. The result was that Sinn Féin got elected in seventy-three of Ireland's 105 constituencies.[126] In Belfast, the Independent Labour Party put forward two candidates and three trade union candidates also ran. The Labour campaign was based on social and economic issues with the National Question being carefully avoided. In the event, Labour polled only a small vote, coming second in all four Belfast constituencies.[127]

The extension of the franchise in Ireland and the re-drawing of electoral boundaries took place in 1919. Proportional representation was introduced for the first time under the Local Government Act of 1919, in time for the 1920 municipal elections.[128] The Labour Party, under the leadership of Thomas Johnson, concentrated its political energies on maximising its vote in the long delayed municipal and Urban Council elections. Labour's programme for the election was decided at a special ILP&TUC Conference in 1919, attended by twenty-two trades councils. Labour demanded medical care, school meals, direct labour and municipal housing schemes. It was rooted in the bread and butter issues facing workers.[129] There was little indication in the programme that in the south west a violent conflict was developing between Republicans and the British military.[130]

In Belfast, the Labour Party put forward a strong panel, fielding twenty-two candidates.[131] In addition, three Socialist, ten Independent Labour and three NAUL (National Amalgamated Union of Labour) candidates ran. The NAUL candidates were supported by their Executive and ran in Woodvale, Victoria, Dock and Pottinger Wards.[132] In the event, ten of the Belfast Labour Party candidates and three other Labour type candidates were elected. This was despite attempts by the Unionist Party to sabotage their chances by running Ulster Unionist Labour Association (UULA) candidates against Labour. The UULA was formed in 1918 from a Watch Committee set up at the time of the Irish Convention. That it was not a genuine Labour organisation is shown by the fact that its representatives failed to tackle social and economic grievances, either inside or outside Parliament.[133] As it turned out, the Unionists fared badly in the 1920 election, losing fifteen seats on the new City Council.[134] Nationally, Labour won 334 seats out of a total of 1,470 successful candidates.[135] In Ulster, the results were Unionists 266 seats, Sinn Féin 83, Nationalists 77 and Labour 90. In Strabane, three Labour Councillors were elected and in Omagh, two National Labour Councillors were returned. Labour had stood in every county in Ireland.[136] It had also got 19.8% of the vote in Ulster (the nine counties pre-Partition).[137]

In Fermanagh, Labour Councillors were elected for the first time.[138] Prior to the election Enniskillen Trades & Labour Council (ET&LC) had taken a decision not to send a delegate to the ILP&TUC conference to discuss the election. This was not because it was disinterested. On the contrary, as early as October 1919 William Clarke appealed to a Labour meeting to support the candidates selected by EL&TC for the Urban Council election.[139] Following that meeting, another was held in Enniskillen in mid-November. The following resolution was put to what was described by the local press as a large audience:

> '1. Congratulations to the British Trade Unionists on their recent election victories, and a call on Irish Trade Unionists to do likewise in the coming elections.
>
> 2. Congratulations to those Councillors, who had supported the implementation of the Profiteering Act.'

The meeting was addressed by a number of speakers including Donnelly (Derry NAUL), who urged those present to vote only for Labour, despite the protestations of Gordon, Nationalist Chairman of the Urban Council, who was present at the meeting. Coburn (Manchester Unity Operative Bricklayers) also spoke, attacking political jobbery and assuring his audience that Labour would not indulge in it, as they had no rich friends to please. Coburn was supported by Rennie of the House & Ship Painters' Association of Manchester. Rennie declared 'What Manchester said in November, Enniskillen will say in January'.[140]

The Labour campaign continued throughout the winter of 1919, with the ET&LC increasing the pressure on sitting Councillors. A key issue was that of improved street lighting, an issue readily conceded by the sitting Councillors with an election in the offing. The Labour campaign reached its climax at a meeting in Enniskillen Town Hall in early January 1920. At the meeting the Labour candidates pledged to work for jobs, housing and decent conditions for workers. Presumably the candidates would have been bound by the same process as other labour candidates throughout Ireland in that, to be endorsed they had to support the agreed programme of the ILP&TUC, be supported by the local trades council, be active trade unionists and sign a pledge to that affect.[141]

It is interesting to note the different approaches of the three speakers present in the Town Hall – the fourth Candidate, Trotter was ill and unable to attend. William Clarke in his opening address pledged to fight for better wages and better houses for the workers. He emphasised that the campaign was not about individual candidates but about the movement behind them, the Labour movement. Frank Carney, second candidate to speak, stated clearly that his policy was Labour He went on to say that he wanted to raise workers above the level of beasts in the field. Mirroring Clarke he said he wanted workers to have a decent wage to enable workers to look after their children. He described previous leaders as having made demands moderately but stated that they had their shoulder to the wheel and meant to keep it to the wheel until Labour came out on top. Carney was followed by Walter Campling who pledged to work with the Labour members and do everything he could in the interest of the workers. He also pledged to oppose any proposal which was to the detriment of the working man but counselled that it would be necessary for Labour and Capital to co-operate as it took brains, money and work to be successful and provide employment for workers. Perhaps a more moderate approach than Clarke or Carney.

The meeting was also addressed by a Johnson, an NAUL. candidate for Pottinger in Belfast and Boyd, a native of Lisbellaw thirty-five years before, but then living in Belfast after having travelled the world. Boyd welcomed Labour's challenge in Fermanagh and wished them well in the election.[142] The Labour candidates who ran in Enniskillen were

| | |
|---|---|
| East Ward: | W. Clarke, Belmore Street, Postman |
| North Ward: | F. Carney, Abbey Street, Fisherman; |
| | W. Campling, Queen Street, Fisherman |
| South Ward: | T. Trotter, Castle Street, Carpenter [143] |

Bernard Keenan, shop manager from Queen Street, also ran as an Independent Labour candidate in the North Ward.[144] Keenan had served for many years in the Royal Inniskilling Fusiliers with the rank of Sergeant. In the 1911 census, he was a Colour Sergeant (Infantry) living with his wife Rebecca at house 42, Queen Street with five children. The family were Catholic.[145] At one stage, he was the Chief Ranger in the Irish National

Foresters, Devenish Branch. There has been some speculation locally that Keenan was also a drill instructor with the Irish Volunteers but this cannot be confirmed. A reference to a B. Keenan is included in a Bureau of Military History Witness Statement by Francis O'Duffy but it is not certain if this is the same Bernard Keenan.[146] One reason for Keenan standing as an Independent may have been that he was not a union member or Trades Council delegate and could not have been officially endorsed by the ET&LC. He was certainly popular as he lifted the highest individual Labour vote in the North Ward.[147]

Along with Campling and Carney, Keenan was elected in North Ward. It is interesting to note that the Nationalist Election Association only supported the candidature of Campling and Carney and not Trotter, Clarke or Keenan. The local Unionist paper in the week before the election referred to the Catholic Church calling on Catholic voters to vote only for Catholic candidates.[148] This could of course have been a spoiler to dissuade voters from deserting their sectarian voting patterns. The question has to be asked why this does not appear to have included Keenan, a Catholic? Around the same time the *Fermanagh Herald* in an editorial expressed concern that Labour voters had been advised to vote only for Labour.[149] Clearly the Labour campaign was unsettling the sectarian camps.

In the election, Keenan got 88 first preference votes. The quota was 61. Campling received 65 votes and Carney was elected on transfers, after receiving 44 votes. In East Ward, Clarke received 54 first preference votes. The quota was 67. He received only three transfers and was not elected. Trotter fared even worse in South Ward with only 30 votes, the quota being 54.[150] Ironically, although proportional representation was seen as giving Labour a better chance of election, in this case, had it not been used, Clarke would have been elected in addition to the other three Councillors. At their first Council meeting in February 1920, Labour, in line with the policy pursued elsewhere, successfully proposed that meetings be held in the evenings to accommodate Councillors who worked during the day.

Interestingly, the *Impartial Reporter*, even though he had not won a seat, expressed concerns that Clarke had persuaded a few Unionist voters in the East and South Wards to imbibe socialism.[151] Labour polled 19.24% of the vote in the Enniskillen Urban Area which closely reflected what happened in the rest of Ulster.[152] Labour was soon, however, to be involved in a more controversial issue. At the March meeting of the Urban Council, a proposal was made by Councillor Carney that an Anti-Partition motion be adopted. A heated debate ensued during which J. Cooper, Unionist, reminded Labour representatives that Protestant voters had supported them as non-political representatives. In any event, the motion was carried by eleven votes to ten, with Unionists opposing and Labour with the Nationalists supporting it.[153] Labour policy at the time was one of opposition to Partition, both Home Rulers and anti-Home Rulers contributing to this policy, albeit for different reasons.[154]

In May 1920, William Clarke was nominated to stand for Labour in the Rural and County Council elections. He was also nominated for the Enniskillen Board of Poor Law Guardians.[155] His candidature was subsequently supported at a Labour Day rally in Enniskillen. held in the Gaol Square. The rally followed a parade of several hundred workers led by the Discharged Soldiers & Sailors Band. At the rally, the Farmers' Union were criticised for their attacks on trade unions. One farmer was singled out, Maguire, a member of the local Board of Poor Law Guardians. It was claimed that while he opposed wage increases for the workers, he had five jobs earning him £675 per year, as well as one hundred acres of land. After a number of resolutions on control of food pricing, tillage and housing were passed, Clarke addressed the meeting. In his speech, he emphasised the importance of voting Labour in the June election and getting him elected to the County Council.[156] Despite the Labour Rally's support for Clarke, his candidature was not well received in Nationalist circles. In late May, the *Fermanagh Herald* made an attack on Clarke. They said

'Mr. W. Clarke has been nominated as a Labour candidate for Enniskillen area and the Board of Guardians. He says he recognises no political party but it is significant that his election address has only been published in the Orange press. Further comment on his candidature is unnecessary.'[157]

Clarke seems to have also fallen foul of former comrades and was also criticised by the ET&LC who repudiated his action in offering himself as a candidate in the local government election and called on him to resign his position as President of the Council.[158] Clarke's fate was sealed when he received only 34 votes in the Poor Law Guardians election, the quota was 160. Likewise, in the County Council Election, he received only 44 votes with a quota of 75. Clarke may have been attacked because, by standing in Enniskillen, he threatened to split the Nationalist vote. Alternatively, perhaps he was just unacceptable as an individual to the Nationalist establishment and perhaps some in the local official labour movement. The attack on Clarke may also have been a sign of the growing sectarianism, which was to engulf the north of Ireland in July 1920.[159]

Despite these setbacks, Labour both in the Urban Council and the ET&LC continued the agitation to improve workers conditions. In April 1920, the ET&LC succeeded in obtaining a ten shilling rise for carters, porters and bakers in Enniskillen after intervening in a dispute. Also in April, the Urban Council gave their workers a ten shilling rise and a half-day holiday on Saturdays, after pressure from Labour Councillors. This will have the been the half day Councillors refused to implement in 1912. On the social and economic front, Labour was campaigning for the improvement of street lighting and the implementation of a scheme to build 300 houses in Enniskillen. It was, however, beginning to meet opposition to its plans.

At the January 1921 meeting of the Urban Council, a Unionist Councillor, George Elliot, Junior, proposed that the decision to call in experts to examine the street lighting be rescinded. At the same meeting, another Unionist Councillor James Cooper proposed that a decision to apply for a Government loan to start the housing scheme be rescinded. On this occasion, both proposals were defeated.[160] In July, Councillor Elliot, proposed that no wage claims be accepted until February 1922, again after Labour opposition, the proposal was defeated.[161]

Fermanagh was now about to experience some of the effects of the sectarian conflict that had raged in Belfast since July 1920. The conflict began after Catholics, socialists and what were described as 'Rotten Prods' (Protestants with Labour sympathies) were expelled from Belfast shipyards by militant Loyalists provoked by their political masters. In a short time, the trouble spread to other industries and residential areas. The violence that ensued was to last two years and cost over three hundred lives.[162] While there were no similar pogroms taking place in Fermanagh, a fund was set up by a local newspaper, the *Fermanagh Herald*, to help expelled workers.[163]

However, in February 1921, a dispute over union membership became the subject of sectarian wrangling. It concerned a situation where workers employed in the construction of a new Co-Operative Bakery objected to working with five non-union members. When approached, four of the five agreed to join the NAUL, but the fifth, a member of the Ulster Workers' Trade Union (UWTU), refused to join. A strike ensued, and allegations of political abuse being directed at the UWTU member by NAUL members were made. Clarke the local NAUL Official, and Sam Bradley, the Irish Official Delegate, both from the Protestant community, denied these allegations.[164] The dispute, nonetheless, continued for a couple of weeks and Turkington, the UWTU leader, launched an attack on the NAUL, using the Conscription issue as ammunition. In the end, it took the intervention of the United Co-Operative Baking Society to resolve the dispute.[165] In any case, while the dispute was settled without recourse to violence, it marked the beginning of a number of setbacks, industrially and politically, for Labour in Fermanagh.

These began in August, when Thomas Cassidy, Irish Organiser, Typographical Association (TA), addressed Fermanagh County Council. He asked them not to accept any tenders from Trimble, a local printer. This action was necessary, Cassidy claimed, because Trimble employed cheap female labour, misused apprentices and did not comply with the fair wages clause. Trimble denied these allegations but Cassidy produced evidence to support his claim from His Majesty's Stationery Office (HMSO). Despite this evidence, however, Trimble won the vote by ten votes to nine, with two abstentions, a setback for the TA locally.[166]

In June 1922, Councillor Carney (Labour) and Councillor Kelly (Nationalist), a local draper, were both disqualified from the Urban Council for non-attendance. Carney had been interned allegedly for his Republican as opposed to his Labour activities. In later years, it transpired that Carney as well being an ex- British soldier retired on medical grounds during the First World War was a member of Michael Collins's Irish Republican Brotherhood (IRB) and an IRA commander in Fermanagh. He was interned but later released and went on to become a respected member of the Fianna Fáil party and a TD.

Clearly the republican movement had a strategy in Enniskillen to capture some of the Labour vote in North Ward when they organised to have Carney put forward as a bona fide Labour candidate. In any case, despite the usual practice of co-opting a replacement, on this occasion the Unionists used the opportunity of an absent Nationalist Councillor, Gordon, to snatch the seat from Labour. Interestingly, Seán Nethercott a Sinn Féin Councillor also tried to claim Carney's seat for the Republicans. Labour's unhappiness with Carney was apparent when, during the debate, another Labour Councillor, Campling, said, 'The Labour Union was about to ask him to withdraw from the Council'.[167]

Undoubtedly these developments were disillusioning for Labour and their supporters across the political divide. Nonetheless, Labour organised itself and bounced back as will be seen later in this narrative. It is indicative of the period that attempts were made to steal Labour's clothes by both Unionists and Republicans.

In any case these developments meant that the Unionists now had ten seats to Labour and the Nationalists nine. This heralded Labour's most serious setback. In July 1922, Councillor Cooper proposed that an application to the Local Government Board for a £66,000 loan to build new housing be cancelled. Before Cooper had proposed the motion, a large body of workmen had marched to the Town Hall and a deputation, led by William Clarke, were allowed into the Council Meeting. Cooper, in opposing the loan, took the view that while there was a need for housing, the town could not afford it. Clarke and the Labour Councillors contended that the present houses were hovels, unfit for human habitation, and new homes should be built whatever the cost. Cooper produced figures which he claimed showed that the town would be bankrupted if the houses were built. The Borough Surveyor contradicted the figures. A long debate ensued, during which charge and counter charge were made. At one stage a compromise was proposed and rejected. In any event, when the vote was taken, twelve voted for Cooper's motion and eight voted against.[168]

Labour became somewhat disheartened after this defeat. In September, Campling was also disqualified for non-attendance. He had been badly injured in the First World War and was in indifferent health at the time and working in the local tax office. He subsequently became a founding member of the British Legion in Enniskillen and committed a lot of his time to looking after the rights of injured war veterans like himself. He died in October 1931 at the age of thirty-four leaving behind a wife and a young family.[169] This left Councillor Keenan as Labour's sole representative on the

Urban Council.[170] With Unionists now holding thirteen seats, Councillor Cooper began to make use of his new-found power. In September, he proposed that the unemployment relief scheme jobs be allocated at the rate of two thirds for Protestants and one third for Catholics – the practice in Belfast.[171] The scheme he referred to was one agreed between the British, Irish and Northern Irish Governments when the Treaty was signed. The scheme provided a sum of £500,000 for relief works in Belfast and its environs. This money, as Councillor Cooper said, was to be allocated at the rate of two thirds to Protestants and one third to Catholics, reflecting the religious make up in the city. Preference was to be given to ex-servicemen in the case of Protestants and Expelled Workers in the case of Catholics. What Councillor Cooper failed to mention was that a grant of £50,000 was also given to areas outside of Belfast for relief works. The only criteria in this case being that preference be given to Expelled Workers and ex-servicemen.[172]

This was a somewhat different picture to that painted by Cooper and was perhaps a sign of things to come. In October 1922, the Urban Council supported the abolition of Proportional Representation (PR) and the introduction of a £10 deposit for future election candidates. By January 1923, twenty-one Unionists had been elected to the Urban Council unopposed. Nationalists had abstained from the election, along with Labour, because re-drawn boundaries meant that, although there were a majority of Nationalists in the urban area, they could only return seven Councillors out of twenty-one. The end of Labour representation in the county came in 1923. A similar situation pertained in the rest of Ulster. Industrially too, Labour was facing serious problems with the onset of economic depression.

Members of the newly-appointed Fermanagh Trades Council, 1978

Fermanagh Council of Trade Unions, 1980s

# 6

## *Facing the Counter Attack:*
## *Economic Boom Collapses*

The post-war economic boom was collapsing in Ireland by 1921. The total number of insured workers unemployed was 114,000 by December. In addition, 20,000 casuals were also unemployed. These figures did not include uninsured workers, such as agricultural labourers and domestic servants. In total 24% of Irish industrial workers were unemployed and 4% were on short time.[173] In Northern Ireland by October 1921, 78,000 people were unemployed and 25,000 on short time. Quite a lot of the unemployment was due to a decline in the traditional staples of shipbuilding and linen.[174] Increasing unemployment led to a decline in union membership, both in Britain and Ireland. The NAUL for example, had a membership of 143,000 in 1920 but by 1923 this had fallen by 63% to 53,000. Other British-based unions faced a similar decline with the Workers' Union losing 69% of their membership in the same period.[175] In Ireland, unions faced a similar decline. While in 1919 nearly 300,000 members were affiliated to the Irish Labour Party & Trades Union Congress (ILP&TUC), by 1921 this had dropped to 190,000.[176] It was in such an atmosphere, with Civil War raging in the south-west and sectarian violence raging in the north, that employers began to attack trade unions and wages. In Belfast, wages in the shipbuilding and engineering industries were slashed by as much as twenty-two shillings a week. Other workers, such as dockers and carpenters experienced similar demands for reductions in wages from three to twelve shillings respectively.[177]

Workers in Fermanagh also faced employer offensives as they tried to claw back the benefits won in the post-war years. In November 1921 building workers from six firms in Enniskillen were locked out after refusing to accept a wage reduction of two shillings and sixpence, and an increase in hours, from 1 January 1922.[178] The dispute was a bitter one, lasting more than twelve weeks. By January 1922 the locked-out workers were under severe pressure and faced attacks from the media, police and the Ulster Workers' Trade Union (UWTU). In late January, two carpenters, Lally and Martin, were taken to Court and fined twenty shillings for following a scab called Armstrong. Fortunately for them, on appeal, the judgement was overturned to the delight of local trade unionists.[179] Nonetheless, such was the opposition being drummed up against worker organisation that it was necessary for the unions to convene a public meeting to counter the misinformation campaign. The meeting was held in Enniskillen Town Hall on 20 January 1922. Workers and their wives were invited to attend so that they might hear the true story of the dispute. Councillor Keenan chaired the meeting, which was addressed by William Clarke and Sam Bradley (National Amalgamated Union of Labour, NAUL) along with Mr Coburn (National Federation of Building Trade Operatives, NFBTO). All three speakers stressed that the dispute was a lockout rather than a strike. Claims that the strike was politically or religiously motivated were vigorously denied. These claims had come from two sources, UWTU leader James Turkington and the *Impartial Reporter*. Turkington in reply to a telegram inviting him to the meeting stated that he 'would be very pleased to reply to honest criticism. Consider present dispute not legitimate, strike only a form of boycott'.

The *Impartial Reporter* implied similar sentiments when it said the builders' meeting was only advertised in a Sinn Féin Omagh paper, a reference to the *Fermanagh Herald*.[180] It was somewhat ironic that a few years earlier the *Fermanagh Herald* had been making the opposite claim against Clarke. The reason no advertisement was placed with the *Impartial Reporter* was because it had been attacking the workers and their leaders for several weeks. Turkington's reference to a boycott concerned a Sinn Féin Boycott of Belfast goods in the wake of the 1920 pogroms. The Belfast Boycott lasted from 1920-1922 and was estimated to have cost Belfast £5 million in lost trade, although it did little to help Expelled Workers.[181] In the case of the Enniskillen dispute, there is absolutely no evidence to suggest that it was anything other than an industrial dispute.

A concerted effort was being made by the establishment and the UWTU to divide the workers on religious and political grounds. Indeed, the NAUL and the NFBTO alleged that the employers were marching scabs down to join the UWTU so keen were they to cause division.[182] In the event, despite attempts at division, the workers won through and in mid-February had settled with four of the six firms involved. Their success is shown by the fact that one of the terms of settlement was that all employees had to join the NFBTO.[183] In other sectors however, there was not as much resistance to wage cutting. In January, local tailors, having at first refused to do so, accepted a reduction of ten shillings a week imposed by the drapers.[184] Likewise, in February, Urban Council workers had their wages reduced by two shillings and sixpence with the threat of a similar cut in May. In June, the Board of Guardians reduced Outdoor Relief payments by a quarter! Then in September, they tried to reduce their workers' wages by fifteen shillings, which would have left them thirty shillings for a seven-day week. On this occasion however, the Guardians were overruled by the Ministry of Commerce.[185]

With the exception of this intervention, no resistance to wage cuts was evident until March 1923, the year which saw the emergence of a new

Building which housed the Labour Hall and T&G Offices,
*Courtesy Pat D'Arcy*

general union in Fermanagh, the Transport & General Workers Union of Great Britain & Ireland (TGWU). The TGWU had been formed in January 1922 by fourteen unions, representing 350,000 workers.[186] The first of its activities in Fermanagh were reported in January 1923. Local newspapers announced that members of the NAUL had joined the TGWU. Their first public meeting was held in the Labour Hall, Enniskillen.

The TGWU meeting was chaired by James Maguire, a local man, and addressed by William Clarke, who had been appointed as TGWU District Organiser. McCurdy, from Belfast, also addressed the meeting and stressed the benefits of joining the union, while emphasising that the union was not interested in politics. He condemned the hoisting of the Red Flag over a Limerick creamery and assured his audience that the TGWU would not be hoisting flags of any type. Clarke, in his address, welcomed the good attendance, and went on to say that the NAUL had done a good job for the workers of Enniskillen, but was now being led astray by Officials who had no spirit of trade unionism. He finished by urging workers to join the new union.[187] Clarke may have been referring to a number of difficulties which affected the NAUL in the 1920s. The dramatic fall in union membership from 143,000 in 1920 to 53,000 in 1923, necessitated cut backs in Officers and Branches. It was also alleged, that some Officers were so keen that the amalgamation ballot was successful, that they rigged ballots in some areas.[188]

Either of these problems may have led to local NAUL members becoming disillusioned and joining the TGWU.

In any event, it was the TGWU who challenged further attempts at reducing the wages of Urban Council workers. On 25 February 1923, Council cleansing staff came out on strike. The strike was in protest against a proposal to reduce their wages from £2 2s 6d to £1 17s, a cut of 5s 6d per week. Workers in the local co-operative mills were also out on strike over similar demands for wage reductions.[189] The battle with the Urban Council was to be the most bitter. The dispute was made official by the TGWU Executive in early March but the Urban Council adopted a hard line. They refused point blank to meet a deputation, which included Clarke. McCurdy, a Belfast Official, attempted to reason with the Council, but to no avail.[190] Three weeks into the dispute there were threats of putting the street cleaning out to tender. Indeed, on the night before Lord Derby visited the town, the Urban Council organised a troop of shopkeepers, prominent citizens, and auxiliary police, to clean the streets. This move was condemned by McCurdy at a TGWU meeting where he announced that offers of help had been made from Belfast, Derry and Dundalk dockers. Workers in Omagh had also pledged support. Allegations that the dispute was political were rejected when E.P. Harte, an Official from Dublin, described the union's politics as 'bread and butter, with a little bit of jam'.[191]

The dispute was at a stalemate, when Councillor Cooper, Unionist leader of the Council, and McCurdy met for talks in Belfast. At the meeting, it was agreed that wages would be reduced to £2 for labourers and £2 5s for carters - a reduction of 2s 6d as opposed to 5s 6d originally proposed. One catch in the agreement, however, was Cooper's refusal to have any future dealings with Clarke.[192] This obviously left Clarke in an impossible position and left no doubt that the establishment were out to silence him and with him they hoped, Labour locally. After the local TGWU Branch insisted that part of the agreement be that all Council workers join the TGWU, the deal fell through. The Council then employed scab labour who had to be escorted through the town by police. Indeed, one worker, Alexander Whittaker, was fined ten shillings for abusing a scab.[193] Despite support from Belfast dockers, who refused to handle goods bound for Enniskillen, the Urban Council refused to concede. As late as June 1923 they refused to meet a deputation made up of E.P. Harte, J. Jones, the local Branch Secretary, and Bernard Keenan, the ex-Labour Councillor.[194] In the final analysis, all that could be secured for the victimised workers was casual jobs, as the Urban Council refused to dismiss the scabs. In November 1923 the TGWU Executive agreed to pay a grant of £5 to the victimised workers and to pursue their re-instatement. Clarke was severely censured by the union for not accepting the original deal although it was the branch rather than Clarke who had refused.[195] Clarke had underestimated the power of the Urban Council in a time of division and unemployment. Had the union been able to hit profits, as was the case in the builder's dispute, the outcome might have been different. In any event, as membership declined, cutbacks in the union led to Clarke losing his full-time position.

1923 was not just a year of doom and gloom though. The union also had its victories. In the long running dispute between the Poor Law Guardians and their ambulance driver, an award was made at Fermanagh assizes for £4 5s in the worker's favour.[196] In April his wages were agreed at £2 10s per week, after the intervention of the Ministry of Commerce, this was £1 more than they wanted to pay and a lot of money to workers at the time.[197] Another victory was achieved by the TGWU when the Branch Secretary Jones succeeded in forcing the Urban Council to compensate workers on the Ballydoolagh water scheme, for a short payment.[198] Other unions also continued their activities, in April, the local INTO Branch became involved in the campaign for a public library in the county.[199]

Fermanagh Council of Trade Unions, 2000s

# 7

## 'No Homes for People or Books' – Labour's Housing Struggle in Fermanagh

The previous chapter finished on a depressing note with the defeat of a strike of Council workers and the isolation of William Clarke. Clarke went on to set up his own bus service in the Fermanagh area and in 1937 was Chairman of the North of Ireland Provincial Hauliers' Association. While addressing a meeting of Hauliers in Enniskillen, he continued to advocate transport workers being organised in a union.[200] He ran again for elected office before the Second World War, this time running as an Independent Unionist against what he saw as the representatives of 'big house Unionism' then prevalent but he was again defeated. Clarke died in August 1950 in Omagh. His obituary records that although not officially involved with the Labour movement, he maintained his Labour convictions to the end.[201]

This chapter picks up on the activities of those comrades of Clarke who were able to continue the struggle for workers in Fermanagh after 1923, concentrating mainly on the activities of William Kelly and John Jones who had campaigned with Clarke after the First World War and into the early 1920s. Kelly was born in 1873 in Mary Street, Enniskillen.[202] According to the 1911 Census, he was living in Strand Street and was a tailor by trade. He was Catholic.[203] Although the Enniskillen Branch of the Amalgamated Society of Tailors and Tailoresses (AST&T) had been in existence since 1856,[204] Kelly's first trade union activity was likely to have been during the 1890 tailors' strike in the town which led to several tailors being jailed after there was some trouble during the dispute.[205] The 1911 Census shows a John Jones living and working along with Henry Jones in Townhall Street, Enniskillen at a local Hotel, where he was employed as a 'Hotel Boots'. His birth place is shown as Liverpool.[206] John and Henry moved back to Monaghan from Liverpool with their family and in 1909 moved on to Enniskillen according to his grandchildren. He was Catholic.

The housing of the working classes had been an issue for many years not just in Enniskillen but throughout the county.[207] In 1915, Councillor Gordon, Nationalist, succeeded in getting a proposal adopted by the Urban Council to build thirty-two new houses. However, it soon ran into trouble when Trimble, Unionist, put forward a motion seeking that the scheme be rescinded on the grounds of cost. Although Trimble's motion was defeated, the proposed housing scheme was never built.[208] It was shelved because the war intervened, after the war the Local Government Board improved the specification on the houses delaying developments and making them more expensive.[209]

While the campaign of Enniskillen Trades & Labour Council (ET&LC) and subsequently that of Kelly and Jones calling for decent housing was a general one, their emphasis was on the

Royal Hotel
*Courtesy Benny Cassidy and Old Enniskillen Facebook Page*

biggest concentration of poor housing at the time in North Ward. This area was known by some locally as the 'back streets' and by others as the 'Dardanelles' because there were fatalities from every street in this area during that military campaign. The Dardanelles were located between Queen Street and Hall's Lane until their demolition in the late 1960s.

The first part of this area to be occupied was Barrack Lane, now called Queen Street where houses were built in 1797. Other streets were developed from 1825 including, Strand Street, Head Street, Mary Street, Abbey Street and Dame Street which formed terraces bounded by Darling Street on the south and an open area called Carleton's Park in the east. By 1842, there was a National School at the corner of Head Street and Dame Street. By 1858 it had moved to Abbey Street and was taken over by the Sisters of Mercy as an infant school in 1905.[210]

In common with the whole island, Land and Labour Leagues had been organised in various areas of Fermanagh campaigning around housing and land rights for labourers during the nineteenth century. Sometimes that agitation had support across the communities and at other times had become the subject of controversy between Nationalists and Unionists.[211] As referred to earlier, in April 1919 the newly formed ET&LC passed a motion from the local NAUL branch drawing their attention to the insanitary housing conditions prevailing in some areas of the town and calling for remedial works before the summer period. The motion referred

### The Dardanelles
*Courtesy Benny Cassidy and Old Enniskillen Facebook Page*

specifically to conditions in Dame Street and Abbey Street where no ash pits were provided to any of the houses except for one communal pit at the lake shore which local children also used as a playground.[212] The ET&LC subsequently forwarded the motion to Enniskillen Urban Council (EUC). They also highlighted insanitary conditions on a range of streets in Enniskillen, including the White Hart, Henry Street, Coleshill Terrace, Queen Street, Abbey Street, Head Street, Strand Street and Mary Street and called for urgent action. The EUC were not happy that their lack of progress was being criticised by working people and the representatives of organised labour.[213]

ET&LC's concerns were well founded when a report in the local press at the start of June 1919 from the EUC's own Housing Committee found that in one area of the town 126 families were housed in 104 houses. The houses in the main were four roomed and earthen floored and many had no fire grates and very poor fireplaces. In another area, forty-two houses were occupied by sixty-four families. Very few of the houses had running water and water was taken from two pumps on the streets. The report concluded by advising the Council that there were currently forty applicants for every vacant house in the urban area.[214]

William Clarke, then local NAUL Organiser, led a deputation to a meeting with the EUC in August 1919 in the wake of a report that 200 families in Enniskillen were poorly housed. As already mentioned above the outcome of the meeting was that the ET&LC could nominate members to the EUC's Housing Committee as advisers.[215] Subsequently in October 1919, the EUC announced a scheme to build 350 new homes.[216]

On Mayday 1920, ET&LC demanded that the Government put housing schemes into operation for both urban and rural workers as well as rewarding the returned soldiers and sailors by granting the houses and land they had been promised for their services to the nation.[217] A few weeks earlier a prominent Councillor and local solicitor showed his support for the housing scheme by proposing that the Council sow oats on the site.[218]

The advent of Partition, abolition of PR and the gerrymandering of Councils ushered in a dark period in the town's political development. It was January 1926 before Labour got publicly involved in the political struggle again when they ran seven candidates in the EUC elections in North Ward. Nationalists had been boycotting the elections for the previous three years. Six of Labour 's nominees were returned unopposed along with a business candidate, J. P. Gillin who had previously run as a Nationalist.

Enniskillen Townhall
*Courtesy Benny Cassidy and Old Enniskillen Facebook Page*

Those returned for labour were John Jones, Corporation Street; William Kelly, Strand Street; Terence Carroll, Darling Street; Patrick Drumm, Castle Street; James Ginn, Market Street; and James Lynn, Castle Street. Again, there was sectarian wrangling as it seems it was expected that Catholic business candidates would receive support in the East and South Wards as a quid pro quo for support from Nationalists for what the Nationalist *Fermanagh Herald* described as 'Protestant Labour' candidates in North Ward. There is no evidence that labour ran candidates on a religious basis but as the results show they did try to have candidates who were representative of both communities.[219] On 25 September 1926 Jones, William Love and John Monaghan attended the Northern Ireland Labour Party conference in Belfast as delegates from ET&LC.[220]

Previous experience had shown Labour that the housing of the working classes, especially those unskilled workers who could not afford high rents was clearly not going to be a priority for EUC and most especially the business elements on the Council. This was not all that surprising given the interests of two of the main opponents, James Cooper and J.F. Browne, had in renting out properties in the county. The Council did build sixteen houses in Coleshill in 1925 but these were the subject of sectarian wrangling when they were all given to Protestant applicants. Although the bias was not purely sectarian, the list of successful applicants shows that the houses were in the main given to Government employees including one person employed by Councillor Cooper. An added factor in the allocation of the houses was that the tenants could afford higher rents than the unskilled working class and were not a 'burden' on the rates.[221]

In December 1926, Labour was again to the fore in the EUC when they highlighted the continuing poor housing conditions that working class people were subject to. Responding to a report from the EUC's Housing Committee which recommended not building new houses because the cheapest house that could be built would still be a burden on the rates. Labour Councillor Jones referred to three small houses in the North Ward where fifty-three people were huddled, with one of the houses having no fewer than twenty-four people living in it. He also highlighted the fact that while the EUC had received Government grants under the Housing of the Working Classes Acts and had built houses for the well to do and moneyed classes, it had not in over twenty years erected a single house suitable for an ordinary unskilled worker. His fellow Labour Councillor William Kelly agreed and advised EUC that in the area where he lived practically every house had been condemned, yet this was also the area where many men had voluntarily gone out to fight the battles for those who refused to provide them with a house in which to reside decently. In the event, EUC opposed Jones's proposal that the Committee report be referred back by a majority of one vote. The arrogance of some of the other Councillors is probably best shown by J.F. Brown, who referring to Jones's contribution said, 'I will reply to Mr Jones by asking why the opposition is here like the Clogher Valley Tram, because it is small and noisy'.[222]

Labour was now affiliated to the Labour Party, Northern Ireland through the Enniskillen Workers' Council and ran candidates in the Local Government Elections for the Enniskillen Board of Poor Law Guardians.[223] John Jones, Corporation Street was nominated for East Ward; Peter O'Neill, Wellington Place, North Ward; and Patrick Drumm, Castle Street. South Ward. O'Neill was returned unopposed in Labour's stronghold of North Ward. Jones and Drumm were both contested. Jones polled 239 votes out of a total of 835 but lost out by 52 votes and two Unionists were elected. Drumm polled 139 votes out of a total of 609 votes and two Unionists were elected. Despite losing narrowly, Jones said, 'Taking everything into consideration I am well satisfied with the result'. Presumably he was pleased to be lifting votes across the community and outside Labour's traditional stronghold of North Ward.[224]

Jones was not deterred by setbacks and in November 1927, the Labour Councillors campaigned to establish an adequate fire service in the town. Jones had raised the issue the previous year, but EUC had taken no action. He was raising it again in the context of a fatality and several injuries in the previous week which left ten children fatherless. Jones and Kelly again faced opposition from Councillors Trimble and Brown but had allies across the chamber from other Unionist Councillors including William Hamilton, JP.[225]

The previous year a recommendation from the Chief Fire Officer for Belfast that EUC buy a new fire engine with adequate capacity for the size of the town, build a fire station and establish a voluntary firefighting team, had been turned down by Council. This time however the Labour Councillors were successful and in the wake of the fatal fire. EUC agreed to get a £2,400 loan to buy a new fire engine, build a fire station and establish a voluntary fire service.[226]

Kelly and Jones campaigned not just on housing issues but in the general industrial area as well. In January 1927, Jones raised the question of holiday pay for Enniskillen workers employed on a road widening scheme and was successful in getting EUC's agreement to pay two days' pay at Christmas. Interestingly some Unionist Councillors supported him and Kelly on a cross community vote against Councillor Trimble, a journalist with the *Impartial Reporter* which his father, William Copeland Trimble, owned. Trimble had opposed the payment on the basis that the men were not permanent workers.[227]

Labour's campaign continued into 1928 on an unlikely issue. In March 1928, after representations from marching bands from both sides of the community, Labour Councillor Kelly moved a motion calling for the rescinding of a law which prohibited the playing of marching bands in the

John Jones
*Courtesy of Marius Jones his Grandson*

streets of Enniskillen between sunset and sunrise, apart from His Majesty's troops. During the debate on the motion Kelly's colleague, John Jones said, 'As far as bands and flags were concerned there was only one he had faith in'. Councillor Trimble responded, 'The Red Flag?' Jones replied, 'The very one!' In the event Kelly's motion was eventually passed.[228] The local nationalist paper, the *Fermanagh Herald*, told its readers in December that bands could now parade anytime they wanted.[229] Whether this was a positive development is open to debate.

In May 1928, Labour Councillors were back in conflict with EUC on industrial issues when they submitted a motion calling on Council to adopt a 'Fair Wages Clause'. The motion was defeated on a vote of five to seven with some Unionist Councillors aligning themselves with Labour. This suggests a split within Unionism locally on some social issues. Jones claimed that only one public body had rejected the Fair Wages Clause put forward by the Northern Ireland Ministry for Home Affairs up to that time.[230]

Later in 1928, during a debate on a report of the EUC Public Health Committee, Kelly and Jones got the opportunity to raise the housing issue again. During the debate, Kelly declared the condition of workers' houses as a 'disgrace to Christianity'. Kelly used the opportunity to distance himself from Nationalism when challenged by Trimble that the Nationalists in power had built less houses than the Unionists. Kelly said, 'We have nothing to do with that. We would criticise them too'.[231] Clearly neither Kelly or Jones were afraid to nail Labour's colours to the mast when necessary. In August, they tried unsuccessfully to have direct labour employed in a new water scheme for the town, this time the conservative elements won the day by eleven votes to six.[232]

Until forced to do so by Labour, EUC had the reputation of never having built any houses for the working classes.[233] There were small numbers of houses built for returning soldiers in Mill Street and for artisans and Government employees in the Coleshill area. However, EUC were not prepared to build houses for the old, the poor, the low paid or the sick, many of whom had been disabled in the First World War fighting for King and Country. Part of the reason for this was sectarian. They did not want to upset the balance of voters in particular wards because it would likely create a permanent Nationalist majority on the EUC. There was another reason. It jumps out from every newspaper report on housing debates that took place during the two decades from 1910. It was the perceived burden on the ratepayers because Councils would have to subsidise decent housing for the working classes even after they had received generous subsidies from Government. Was this reluctance to pay for decent housing just confined to the bigger Unionist ratepayers or did it apply equally to the bigger Nationalist ratepayers? Perhaps this is what Kelly was alluding to in his response to Trimble's jibes at the meeting in July 1928

By the end of 1928 Jones and Kelly were back into the campaign for housing when the Medical Inspector's Report, while giving a favourable view of the town in general, highlighted major problems in some areas. It reported that 'there were a considerable number of defective and insanitary houses in some districts, Dame Street, Abbey Street, Mary Street, Head Street, Strand Street, Frith's Alley, Cooney's Court and Castle Place'. These areas' issues had been highlighted nearly ten years earlier but still not dealt with. He went on, 'Most of the houses in Cooney's Court are stables which had been converted into human dwellings'. The report also noted that while the EUC had recently erected twenty-eight new dwelling houses there was a need to erect new houses suitable for the working class by taking advantage of the present liberal subsidy provided by Government. Jones and Kelly were critical of the EUC and Kelly claimed that Enniskillen was the only town in Northern Ireland which had not had a housing scheme for the working classes.[234]

In 1929, Jones and Kelly were returned to EUC again in North Ward. Kelly had the second highest vote in the ward of 356 with Jones coming in fifth with 328 votes. Drumm narrowly missed being elected by a margin of thirty-three.[235] In April, housing in Enniskillen was raised in the Northern Ireland Parliament when Joseph Devlin, Nationalist MP for Belfast West, moved a motion calling for an enquiry into the Housing Acts (Northern Ireland). In the debate Cahir Healy, Nationalist MP for South Fermanagh, raised the question of EUC building affordable housing for those in need and echoed the view of the Independent Unionist Councillor for Ballinamallard.[236] Captain Verschoyle who stated that EUC would only act when compelled to do so.[237] February witnessed the Labour Councillors arguing for a home for the local library against stiff opposition from other councillors which prompted Councillor Kelly to say, 'It is my opinion that this council does not intend to house people or books'.[238] In 1929, a Labour Government took office in Westminster. Jones proposed that EUC send a telegram of congratulations to Prime Minister Ramsay Mac Donald on his victory. Unsurprisingly, EUC did not support his proposal.[239]

In February 1930, a major Labour meeting in Enniskillen Town Hall was organised by the Amalgamated Transport & General Workers' Union (ATGWU).[240] The well attended event was addressed by Sam Kyle, a senior ATGWU Officer and previously a NILP MP at Stormont for North Belfast. He attacked the local Chamber of Commerce's criticism of the Labour Government introducing unemployment benefit and commented on employment, the cost of food and the need for decent housing in Fermanagh. He was followed by George Gillespie, ATGWU Irish Secretary, who related his own experience as a docker thirty years before working a thirteen-hour day. He extolled the virtues of the organisation which had brought this exploitation to an end. Also present were representatives of the Derry and Omagh Branches who were fulsome in their praise of the organising skills of John Jones. Kelly, Enniskillen Secretary, National Union of Tailor & Garment Workers and Chair, Enniskillen Labour Party, also attended. Jones paid tribute to Kelly and related how the local Tailors' Branch had been formed in 1856 and how in 1890 two of their members were imprisoned during a dispute about pay cuts. Interestingly the owners of the liberal Unionist *Fermanagh Times* and the Nationalist *Fermanagh Herald* were present because it was said they employed trade union labour. Representatives of the *Impartial Reporter* did not attend. The public meeting was followed by a social evening in the Imperial Hotel.[241]

This was to be one of William Kelly's last public events. On 22 March 1930, the *Fermanagh Herald* reported that on the motion of Jones, James Bradley was unanimously co-opted to EUC to replace the late William Kelly.[242] The EUC, other public bodies and even his political opponents paid tribute to his work and energy. He had died on 22 February 1930 of heart disease in his home in Strand Street, the area he had worked so hard for. Councillor Kelly was given a full civic funeral with the EUC Mace Bearer, Borough Surveyor and Town Sergeant marching in front of the hearse and a large attendance of local people to the nearby Convent cemetery.[243]

In May 1930, EUC finally agreed to erect new houses in the Dardanelles. On 3 May, the *Fermanagh Herald* announced that fifteen new houses were to be built, three in Mary Street and twelve in Strand Street. The houses were to have a rent of five shillings and sixpence making them more affordable to the unskilled worker. The cost to the rates was estimated at two-pence in the £. The houses would contain four rooms, two upstairs and two down with a water supply and a water closet. They would cost £350 each to build and a Government subsidy of £100 could be claimed towards their building. The new Labour Councillor Bradley tried to get the EUC to agree to a lower rent but ultimately it was agreed to go ahead with the scheme with an estimated rent of five shillings and sixpence.[244]

Even though it looked like at last a little progress was being made, it was not long before controversy arose again. In October 1930, A.V. Ashe, Inspector with the Ministry of Home Affairs, came to Enniskillen to hold an enquiry into the application by EUC for a loan of £2,842 to build the houses. By this time the number of houses to be built had been reduced from fifteen to ten and the conservatives on EUC were still opposing this minimal scheme. Councillor F.R. Browne was particularly vociferous perhaps because as a private landlord himself he was renting out twenty-seven houses. The figures revealed at the enquiry showed that EUC had only built forty-two houses since 1890.[245] The only reason any houses were being built now was that the health authorities were about to close ten houses including three in Cooney's Court (the converted stables mentioned earlier). Despite the conservatives, the scheme went ahead and in December 1930 EUC placed tenders in the local press for the erection of the ten houses.[246] Early in 1931, Bradley again raised the question of housing and pledging to fight any attempt to raise the rent of the new houses beyond five shillings and sixpence.[247]

On 27 April 1931, John Jones died of heart failure in his home at Corporation Street. He was forty-six years old and on his death certificate his occupation was listed as Secretary, Workers' Union.[248] The local paper describes his funeral to the convent cemetery. Like his long-time comrade William Kelly he was accorded a full civic funeral attended by a large congregation in recognition of his efforts on behalf of Enniskillen's working class.[249] John Monaghan of Abbey Street was co-opted to Jones's Council seat in May.[250]

In September, there was another heated debate at EUC when it was agreed that they would have to apply for a supplemental loan of £950 to meet additional costs for the houses being erected at Strand Street and Mary Street. Ironically £500 of this was caused by a reduction in Government funding because the Council had not applied soon enough for the grant assistance. As this was going to add 21/2d in the £ to the rates there was a call from the conservative elements to increase the rents. This was opposed by Bradley.[251]

In January 1932, a motion was put forward by Unionist Councillor George Elliot (Junior) that the rents be increased from five shillings and sixpence to seven shillings. A heated debate followed but a vote on party lines of thirteen to seven (five Nationalists, two Labour) saw the increase carried. At this meeting the houses were also allocated to ten local people: Austin Wardsman; a baker, P. McKeown; James Fitzpatrick from Wellington Place; Patrick Smyth, from Castle Place; James Dolan from Head Street; Mrs Mc

Street Signs for Jones Cottages & Kelly's Cottages,
*Courtesy Bernadette Layden, Jim Ledwith and the Crow's Nest Bar*

Mahon, William Vaughan, and William Hicks from Castle Island; J. Mc Cullion and Charles Mc Caffrey, Head Street. Three reserves were also selected: Henderson, Bell and Wildman.[252]

The EUC had at last been forced to build decent houses in the Dardanelles in Labour's stronghold of North Ward. On 2 May 1932, on the back of a letter from Labour Councillor Bradley and supported by John Monaghan, EUC agreed that the new houses at Mary Street should be named Jones Cottages and those at Strand Street, Kelly's Cottages. The EUC agreed unanimously to the proposal.[253] The two streets were demolished between 1968 and 1969 during redevelopment of the area which pulled this old working-class community from their roots.

Jim Browne Memorial Banner at Belfast May Day Parade

# Conclusion

Workers in Fermanagh were combining from as early as 1826. In these early days, this would have been in the craft and friendly societies as combinations were illegal. Fermanagh workers were nevertheless prepared throughout the nineteenth century to take on bad employers to enforce their rights. From the Erne Improvement strike in May 1844 to the 1890 tailors' strike which felt the full force of the law when tailors were jailed on flimsy evidence, workers showed they were prepared to organise and fight for their rights.

From the end of the First World War until 1923, Fermanagh Labour developed in the light of four main factors. The economic boom caused by the War, especially in agriculture, and the resultant dramatic increase in trade union membership, especially amongst unskilled workers, led to unprecedented political support for Labour in the 1920 municipal elections. Finally, the impact of Civil War and sectarian conflict, allied to economic depression, reversed Labour's fortunes. What was the pattern of these developments?

The war and the economic boom increased employment prospects, leading to a reduction in emigration. As Fermanagh was predominantly agricultural, farmers benefited from the agricultural boom. and, because of compulsory tillage regulations, they employed more labourers. The labourers, while they gained employment, saw prices rise much faster than wages. This situation, combined with an enhanced bargaining position caused by a shortage of labour, made them more amenable to union organisation. The same was true of town labourers, who also experienced price increases without equivalent wage rises. Existing union organisation in the county being either craft or industrial was not equipped to cater for the unskilled. They did not, however, desert the unskilled. William Clarke, a member of the Postmen's Federation, set about organising the labourers. It seems likely that Clarke made contact with the labourers through the local Labour Club, which had the aim of organising all workers, skilled or unskilled.

The National Amalgamated Union of Labour (NAUL) was chosen to organise these workers rather than the Irish Transport & General Workers' Union (ITGWU) because the north of Ireland had been mainly the preserve of British based-unions. This was true of Fermanagh, largely because Protestant workers were suspicious of Dublin-based unions, who often had close links with Irish nationalism. The NAUL had a significant base in Belfast and Derry before coming to Fermanagh and had established organisation in Omagh and Strabane. This made it easier for them to establish a base in Fermanagh than other general unions.

Initially the NAUL confined their organisational drive to Enniskillen, presumably because it had an existing trade union base. In addition, it would have been much easier to organise larger groups of labourers employed by local builders or the Council, than it would have been to organise small, scattered groups of farm labourers. The eventual drive into the countryside was undoubtedly influenced by the ITGWU campaign further south, as well as the danger of unorganised farm labourers coming into the towns and driving down the wages of unionised workers. The main reason for the short-lived success of organisation in the countryside, was the agricultural recession which hit in 1920.

The organisation of the urban general worker was more successful for a number of reasons because a percentage of them were in relatively secure employment - for example, those employed by local councils and the gas works. These provided a core of trade union members who would have encouraged membership among casuals taken on at busy periods. The same would have been true in the building trade, where tradesmen with a tradition of organisation, would have encouraged membership amongst the unskilled and casual workers. This trend fits in largely with the national picture, where it was easier to maintain union organisation in the towns and cities, than the countryside.

The development of Enniskillen Trades & Labour Council (ET&LC) followed a similar trend. It was founded at a time when trades councils were being established across Ireland. The activities and success of the NAUL had demonstrated what solidarity amongst workers could achieve. Their struggles also raised workers' expectations so they began to look at the other factors affecting their living standards such as housing, food prices and sanitation. This ultimately led to unions combining in the ET&LC to pursue these broader issues. The Irish Labour Party & Trades Union Congress (ILP&TUC) encouraged the ET&LC, along with those in Omagh and Derry. These influences mirror the pattern of trades councils all over the country at that time.

In terms of activity, however, there were important differences between Fermanagh and elsewhere. Whilst ET&LC campaigned on the broad social and economic issues, it did not appear to have got involved in the great national issues of the time. For example, there is no evidence of its involvement in the Motor Permits Dispute or the political prisoners dispute which many southern trades councils participated in. Their avoidance of these issues was undoubtedly due to the need to maintain unity amongst Catholic and Protestant workers.

The ET&LC's experience of campaigning on social and economic issues no doubt led to a realisation of the need for political power. This was a factor in their decision to put forward candidates in the 1920 municipal elections. Again, this decision would have been influenced by the decision of Labour nationally to stand for election after division on the issue of elections for many years. In the 1920 election, Labour in Fermanagh concentrated on the bread and butter issues affecting workers and avoided the National Question. This reflected the approach by Labour nationally and especially in Ulster, during that election. Although when elected, Labour became involved in a controversy about Partition, this was an isolated incident. In the main, Labour concentrated on social and economic issues directly affecting local workers. While on the Urban Council, Labour allied itself with the anti-Unionists but there were occasions when their alliances included the less conservative Unionist Councillors. The greatest support for Labour Councillors came from North Ward, a mainly Nationalist working class area. In 1920, Labour had only three Councillors out of a total of twenty-one and so, in order to achieve anything so they had to find allies. Very often this was with Nationalists but on occasions it was with both. In later years, under the leadership of Jones and Kelly, a more independent line developed. In the run up to the 1920 election, the trend in Fermanagh did not fit in with the rest of the country. In the south it was not unusual to find Labour and the Nationalists supporting each other in the election. In the north, and certainly in Belfast, Labour remained independent. Fermanagh seems to have fallen in between these two trends. In the 1920 election two Labour candidates were supported by the Nationalists, two by ET&LC and one received no official support from either group. It is also interesting to note that the five Labour candidates reflected closely the proportion of Catholics and Protestants in the town; two Protestant and three Catholic. This practice continued in later Council and Poor Law Guardian elections that Labour was involved with throughout the 1920s.

The election results, however, did not show the same equity, in that the three candidates elected were from Catholic backgrounds, although Clarke did come close to being elected. This may suggest that the Catholic working class were more amenable to Labour politics than the Protestant working class. This analysis, however, must be qualified by taking into account the Unionist party's tactic of tainting Labour as having a Sinn Féin tail. This tactic is bound to have clouded the minds of some Protestant workers. Likewise, the support of the Nationalist Election Association for some Labour candidates is unlikely to have convinced Protestant voters of Labour's independence. Interestingly though it did not deter both communities from getting involved with Labour and in the late 1920's where we see Labour Councillors from both communities sitting on the Council albeit in a situation where Nationalist Councillors were boycotting the election to the by then Gerrymandered councils.

As Civil War and sectarian conflict developed, Labour's fortunes declined dramatically, both politically and industrially. In the south, the National

Question took centre stage, and in the north Unionists began to establish their supremacy. The effects of these developments were also felt in Fermanagh, firstly in a gradual way as Unionists seized vacant seats on the Urban Council and then more dramatically as Unionists took control of all the Urban Council seats when Nationalists abstained in the 1923 election. Labour because they had only three seats were rendered powerless. To have participated in the election would have made no difference as they would have been condemned to perpetual opposition in a gerrymandered council where Unionists held two thirds of the seats.

The industrial situation was similar. Depression and wage cuts were the order of the day. Trade union membership peaked in 1920 and then began to decline. In Fermanagh wage reductions were demanded, and although workers fought such cuts, unemployment and depression undermined their struggle. Trade union membership declined in the county and William Clarke lost his full-time position in the TGWU because area membership could no longer justify a full-time position.

Sectarianism raised its ugly head in Fermanagh Labour. Although sectarian violence had been raging in Belfast from 1920, Labour in Fermanagh had remained fairly unscathed. That was, until the intervention of the Ulster Workers' Trade Union in a number of disputes. Their role, as was the case everywhere, was to divide the workers along religious lines in order to disrupt industrial action. In the event, this appendage to the Unionist Party does not appear to have been very successful in Fermanagh, although it did pick up some members.

Fermanagh Labour was not bowed after 1923 and continued its industrial struggles. In 1926, it again entered the political field fighting for better housing and social conditions to complement its industrial campaigning. A small but significant social victory was won when Jones and Kelly got houses built in North Ward. But that is not the end of the story. In our next publication, those who carried the Red Flag forward into the twentieth century in equally difficult conditions on behalf of working people will be revealed.

# Bibliography

**Primary Sources**

NAUL Executive Minutes, GMB College, Manchester (now deposited in the Modern Records Centre, Warwick University, Coventry)

NAUL Quarterly and Annual Reports, GMB College, Manchester (now deposited in the Modern Records Centre, Warwick University, Coventry)

TGWU Executive Minutes, Transport House, London (now deposited in the Modern Records Centre, Warwick University, Coventry)

RIC. Monthly Reports, Public Record Office, London, CO 904

1926 Census, Northern Ireland Statistics & Research Agency.

1911 Census, http://www.census.nationalarchives.ie/

Bureau of Military History, 1913-21, WS Ref # 654, Francis O'Duffy, Captain IV, Enniskillen, PRONI


**Newspapers & Journals**

ILP & TUC, Annual Reports, 1919 and 1928 (see http://centenaries-ituc.national archives.ie/annual-reports/)

Board of Trade, *Labour Gazette*, 1922, Ruskin College Library, Oxford

*Irish Opinion*, National Library of Ireland, Dublin

*Fermanagh Herald*, Enniskillen Library

*Impartial Reporter*, Enniskillen Library

*Fermanagh Times*, Enniskillen Library

*Enniskillen Chronicle & Erne Packet*, Enniskillen Library

*Nation*, (Online)

*Donegal Independent*, (Online)

*Fermanagh Mail*, Enniskillen Library

*Ulster Herald*, (Online)

*Irish Opinion*, Dublin, National Library

*Irish Times*, (Online)

*Watchword of Labour*, Irish & Local Studies Library, Armagh


**Published Sources**

Bagwell, Philip S. *The Railwaymen, vol 1*, (Allen & Unwin, London, 1963).

Boyd, Andrew, *Rise of the Irish Trade Unions, 1729-1970*, (Anvil Books, Tralee, 1972)

Buckland, Patrick. *Irish Unionism 2, Ulster*, (Gill & Macmillan, Dublin, 1972)

Clarkson, Jesse Dunsmore. *Labour and Nationalism in Ireland*, (Columbia University, New York, 1925)

Clegg, Hugh A. *General Unions in a Changing Society*, (Blackwell & Mott, Oxford, 1964)

Cunningham, John. *The Great Silence. The Famine in Fermanagh, 1845-1850*, (Davog Press, Enniskillen, 2012).

Devine. Francis & Smethurst, John B. *Historical Directory of Trade Unions in Ireland*, (Irish Labour History Society/Working Class Movement Library, Dublin/Salford, 2017)

Fitzpatrick, David. 'Strikes in Ireland. 1914-1921', *Saothar 6*, 1981, pp.26-39.

Greaves, C. Desmond. *The Irish Transport and General Workers Union: The Formative Years 1909-1923,*(Gill and Macmillan, Dublin, 1982)

Kennedy, Liam & Ollerenshaw, Philip. A*n Economic History of Ulster, 1820-1939,* (Manchester University Press. Manchester, 1985)

Kenny, Bob. *The Spatial Dimensions of Trade Union Organisation in Ireland, A Case Study,* unpublished MA Geog, St Patrick's College Maynooth, 1979.

Livingstone, Patrick. *The Fermanagh Story*, (Cumann Seanchais, Chlocair, 1969)

McCabe, Conor. 'The Irish Labour Party and the 1920 elections', *Saothar 35*, 2010, pp. 22-33

McCarthy, Charles. *Trades Unions in Ireland, 1894-1960*, (Institute of Public Administration, Dublin, 1977)

Mitchell, Arthur. *Labour in Irish Politics, 1890-1930*, (Irish University Press, Dublin, 1974)

O'Connell, T.J. *One Hundred Years of Progress, The Story of the Irish National Teachers Organisation, 1868-1968*, (INTO, Dublin, 1968)

O'Connor, Emmet. *A Labour History of Ireland, 1824-2000*, (University College Dublin Press, Dublin, 2011)

Patterson, Henry. *Class Conflict and Sectarianism, The Protestant Working Class in the Belfast Labour Movement, 1868-1920*, (Blackstaff Press, Belfast, 1980)

Postgate, R.W. *The Builders' History*, (NFBTO, London, 1923)

Redmond, Seán. *The Irish Municipal Employee's Trade Union, 1883-1983*, (IMETU, Dublin, 1983)

Townsend. Charles. 'The Irish Railway Strike of 1920', *Irish Historical Studies*, vol xxi1, no 83, March 1979, pp. 265-282.

TGWU, *The Story of the TGWU*, (TGWU, London, 1975)

Trimble, William C. *The History of Enniskillen*, (Trimble , Enniskillen, 1919)

Vaughan, W.E. & Fitzpatrick, A.J. *Historical Statistics, Population*, (Royal Irish Academy, Dublin, 1978)

Walker, Graham S. *The Politics of Frustration, Harry Midgely and the Failure of Labour in Northern Ireland*, (Manchester University Press, Manchester, 1985)

Wood, H.L. *Enniskillen, Historic Images of an Island Town*, (Friars Bush Press, Belfast, 1990)

# Notes

1   Peadar Livingstone, *The Fermanagh Story*, (Cumann Seanchais Chlocair, Eniskillen, 1969).
2   William Copeland Trimble, *The History of Enniskillen*, (Trimble, Enniskillen, 1919).
3   Jim Quinn, 'Labouring in the margins: trade union activity in Enniskillen, 1917-1923', *Saothar 15*, 1990, pp. 57-64.
4   Jim Quinn "No homes for people or books: Labour's housing struggles in Enniskillen, 1915-1932' in Seán Byers & Francis Devine (eds), *William Walker, 1870-1918: Belfast Labour Unionist Centenary Essays*, (Umiskin Press, Dublin, 2018), pp. 157-168.
5   1926 Census Northern Ireland Statistics and Research Agency (Histpop).
6   W.E. Vaughan & A.J. Fitzpatrick, *Irish Historical Statistics: Population*, (Royal Irish Academy, Dublin, 1978), pp.325-350.
7   *ibid*, pp.67-71
8   D.W. Fitzpatrick, 'The geography of Irish Nationalism 1910-1921', *Past & Present*, No 78, (Feb 1978), pp128
9   *Fermanagh Herald*, 29 October 1921.
10  Fitzpatrick, 'The geography of Irish Nationalism', *op. cit.*, p. 138.
11  *Fermanagh Herald*, 21 January 1922.
12  *Fermanagh Herald*, 24 January 1920.
13  Graham Walker, *The Politics of Frustration, Harry Midgley and the Failure of Labour in Northern Ireland*, (Manchester University Press, Manchester, 1985), pp. 18-19.
14  *Enniskillen Chronicle & Erne Packet*, 23 March 1826
15  *The Enniskillener*, 29 May 1834.
16  See Mel Doyle, 'Belfast and Tolpuddle : attempts at strengthening a trade union presence, 1833-1834', pp.2-12, *Saothar 2*, 1975, pp. 2-12.
17  *The Irishman*, 15 March 1876.
18  *Impartial Reporter*, 30 May 1844.
19  *Enniskillen Chronicle & Erne Packet*, 30 April,1846.
20  John Cunningham, *The Great Silence: The Famine in Fermanagh 1845-1850*, (Davog Press, Belleek, 2012), p. 5.
21  *Fermanagh Herald*, 1 February 1930.
22  Francis Devine & John B. Smethurst, *Historical Directory of Trade Unions in Ireland*, (Irish Labour History Society/Working Class Movement Library, Dublin/Salford, 2017), p305
23  McCarron, 1851-1918, was ASTT Derry Branch Secretary in the early 1890s and imprisoned after a strike. He was elected to the ITUC Parliamentary Committee, 1894-1910, and as President in 1899, 1907 and 1910 He joined the Labour Representation Committee and, after 1912, the Irish Labour Party, and was elected Alderman to Derry City Council and Chair, Public Health Committee. He represented Labour on the Irish Convention, 1917-1918.
24  *Impartial Reporter*, 15 May 1856.
25  *Nation*, 24 December 1864.
26  *Fermanagh Mail & Chronicle*, 16 January 1865.
27  *Impartial Reporter*, 18 March 1880.
28  *Donegal Independent*, 2 June 1888.
29  *Fermanagh Mail*, 30 July1890.
30  *Fermanagh Herald*, 25 February 1905.
31  National Census of Ireland 1911, www.census.nationalarchives.ie
32  *Impartial Reporter*, 13 September 1906.
33  *Fermanagh Herald*, 18 January 1908.

34  *Impartial Reporter*, 8 August 1908.
35  *Fermanagh Herald*, 7 May 1904.
36  *Impartial Reporter*, 25 July 1907.
37  *Fermanagh Herald*, 25 January 1908.
38  *Fermanagh Herald*, 11 April 1908.
39  *Fermanagh Herald*, 12 September 1908.
40  *Fermanagh Herald*, 9 May 1908.
41  *Fermanagh Herald*, 10 October 1908.
42  *Fermanagh Herald*, 17 October 1908.
43  *Fermanagh Herald*, 25 July 1912.
44  *Fermanagh Herald*, 9 March 1912.
45  Charles McCarthy, *Trades Unions in Ireland, 1894-1960*, (IPA, Dublin, 1977), p.31 and C.D. Greaves, *The Irish Transport and General Workers Union: The Formative Years, 1909-1923*, (Gill & Macmillan, Dublin 1982).
46  P.S. Bagwell, *The Railwaymen, Volume One*, (Allen & Unwin, London 1963), p.345.
47  Liam Kennedy & Philip Ollerenshaw, *An Economic History of Ulster, 1820-1939*, (Manchester University Press, Manchester, 1985).
48  Bob Kenny, *The Spatial Dimensions of Trade Union Organisation in Ireland: A Case Study*, (unpublished MA, St Patrick's College, Maynooth,1985).
49  ITGWU, *Annual Report for 1919*, where the list of branches shows very few in Ulster
50  *Fermanagh Herald*, 14 April 1917
51  T.J. O'Connell, *One Hundred Years of Progress, The Story of the Irish National Teachers' Organisation, 1868-1968*, (INTO, Dublin 1968).
52  *Fermanagh Herald*, 23 June 1917.
53  *Fermanagh Herald*, 20 October 1917.
54  David Fitzpatrick, 'Strikes in Ireland, 1914-21', *Saothar 6*, 1980, pp26-39.
55  *Fermanagh Times*, 10 January 1918.
56  Hugh A. Clegg, *General Unions in a Changing Society*, (Blackwell, Oxford,1964), p.26.
57  *ibid*, p.63
58  NAUL Quarterly and Annual Reports 1918, Modern Records Centre, Warwick University (originally consulted in GMB Education Centre, Whalley Range, Manchester).
59  *Fermanagh Times*, 20 February 1918.
60  Greaves, *op.cit*, p.188.
61  Clarkson, *op.cit.*, p.330.
62  *Fermanagh Herald*, 20 April 1918.
63  www.census.nationalarchives.ie
64  *Fermanagh Herald*, 27 April 1918.
65  *Fermanagh Herald*, 19 February 1921.
66  *Fitzpatrick, Saothar, op. cit*, p.31.
67  *Fermanagh Times*, 7 November 1918.
68  *Impartial Reporter*, 7 December 1918.
69  NAUL Executive Minutes, 191
70  *Fermanagh Herald*, 26 October 1918.
71  Greaves, *op. cit*, p. 88,
72  Kenny, *op. cit*, p.56.
73  Francis Devine, 'The ITGWU in Ulster 1918-130', unpublished paper. The numbers were the Head Office Branch registrations numbers, thus Lisnaskea was the 185th branch registered and Newtownbutler the 202nd.
74  *Fermanagh Times*, 31 October 1918.
75  RIC Monthly Reports, Public Record Office, London, C.O.904
76  *Fermanagh Herald*, 29 March 1919.
77  *Fermanagh Herald*, 8 May 1920.
78  *Fermanagh Herald*, 15 March,1919.

79  NAUL Executive Minutes, November 1918

80  NAUL Executive Minutes, January 1919

81  In the newspaper reports the AUCCAW is listed as the Co-Operative and Commercial Employees. The union had been known as the Amalgamated Union of Co-operative Employees until 1917.

82  *Fermanagh Herald*, 1 March 1920.

83  *Fermanagh Herald*, 11 October 1919. The Postal Telegraph Society was most probably the Postal & Telegraph Clerks' Association which was about to become a founding element of the Union of Post Office Workers, today the Communications Workers' Union (UK). The Manchester Unity of Bricklayers, also known as the Manchester Unity of Operative Bricklayers Society, claimed origins from 1829. In 1921, it finally merged with its London equivalent and, joined by the Operative Society of Masons, forming the Amalgamated Union of Building Trade Workers (AUBTW) in 1921. The Manchester Alliance of Operative House Painters was founded in 1856, In 1886, it became the National Amalgamated Society of Operative House Painters and Decorators and, in 1904, the National Amalgamated Society of Operative House & Ship Painters & Decorators (NASOHASPAD). It shortened its title to the National Society of Painters and in 1970 merged with the Amalgamated Society of Woodworkers. In 1971, with the AUBTW, it became a founding part of UCATT (Union of Construction, Allied Trades and Technicians) which in 2017 became part of Unite.

84  Emmett O'Connor, *A Labour History of Ireland, 1824-2000*, (UCD Press, Dublin 2011), p. 36.

85  McCarthy, *op, cit.* p.111.

86  ILP&TUC, *Annual Report 1919*.

87  *Irish Opinion*, 26 January 1918.

88  *Fermanagh Herald*, 22 March 1919.

89  R.W. Postgate, *The Builders' History*, (NFBTO, London, 1923). pp.423-427

90  *Impartial Reporter*, 29 March 1919.

91  *Fermanagh Herald*, 26 April 1919.

92  *Fermanagh Herald*, 12 April 1919.

93  www.census.nationalarchives.ie

94  *Fermanagh Herald*, 4 October 1941.

95  Seán Redmond, *The Irish Municipal Employee's Trade Union, 1883-1983*, (IMETU, Dublin, 1983), p. 44.

96  *Fermanagh Herald*, 26 April 1919.

97  *Fermanagh Herald*, 12 July 1919.

98  *Fermanagh Herald*, 7 June 1919.

99  *Fermanagh Herald*, 18 October 1919.

100 *Irish Times*, 24 November 1919.

101 *Fermanagh Herald*, 11 October 1919.

102 Kennedy & Ollerenshaw, *op. cit*, p.185.

103 *Fermanagh Herald*, 20 December 1919.

104 *Saothar 5*, 1979, back cover illustration

105 *Fermanagh Herald*, 10 May 1919.

106 Clarkson, *op. cit.*, pp 124-128. For UWTU see Devine & Smethurst, *op. cit.*, p. 484.

107 *Fermanagh Times*, 15 May 1919.

108 RIC Monthly Reports, Public Record Office, London, C.O.904

109 NAUL Executive Minutes, June 1919.

110 *Fermanagh Herald*, 27 September,1919.

111 *Fermanagh Herald*, 4 October 1919.

112 NAUL Executive Minutes 27 February 1920.

113 *Fermanagh Herald*, 20 March 1954.

114 *Fermanagh Herald*, 4 October 1919.

115 Postgate, *op. cit.*, p..438.

116 *Fermanagh Times*, 14 October 1918.

117 *Fermanagh Herald*, 16 November 1918.

118 Conor McCabe, 'The Irish Labour Party and the 1920 elections', *Saothar 35*, 2010, pp. 23-33.

119 Walker, *Midgley, op. cit.*, pp. 19-20.

120 Charles Townsend, 'The Irish Railway Strike of 1920', *Irish Historical Studies*, vol XX1, no 83, March 1979, pp. 265-282.

121 *Fermanagh Herald*, 17 June 1920.

122 *Fermanagh Herald*, 24 July 1920.

123 *Fermanagh Herald*, 28 August 1920.

124 *Fermanagh Herald*, 4 March 1922.

125 ILP&TUC, *Annual Report 1919.*

126 Clarkson, *op. cit.*, p338

127 Arthur Mitchell, *Labour In Irish Politics, 1890-1930*, (Irish University Press, Dublin, 1974), p. 101.

128 Patrick Buckland, *Irish Unionism: Volume 2, Ulster*, (Gill & Macmillan, Dublin, 1973), p. 137.

129 Greaves *op. cit.*, p.257.

130 Mitchell, *op. cit.*, p.122

131 *ibid*, p.125

132 NAUL Executive Minutes, 10 January 1920

133 Henry Patterson, *Class Conflict & Sectarianism; The Protestant Working Class & The Belfast Labour Movement, 1868-1920*, (Blackstaff, Belfast, 1980), pp. 97-100.

134 Mitchell, *op. cit.*, pp. 122 ff.

135 McCabe, '1920 elections', *op. cit.*

136 *Watchword of Labour* 31 January,1920.

137 *PR Urban Elections in Ulster 1920*, (The Electoral Reform Society of Great Britain and Ireland, London 1972), p.16.

138 *Fermanagh Herald*, 24 January 1920.

139 *Fermanagh Herald*, 25 October 1919.

140 *Fermanagh Herald*, 15 November 1919.

141 McCabe, '1920 elections', *op. cit.*

142 *Fermanagh Times*, 8 January 1920. In the Census, only one Fermanagh-born William Boyd can be traced living in Belfast. In 1901, William, 46, general labourer, and Church of Ireland, lived with his wife Cassie, 28, and children Maggie, 7, and John, 2, at 19.2 Union Place, St Anne's Ward, Belfast, www.census.nationalarchives. ie/reels/nai000315068/. In 1911, William, 51, general labourer, lived with Catherine, 46, linen doffer, and their children John, 12, Edward, 8, and Maggie, 6, at 27.1 Alexander, East Belfast, www.census.nationalarchives.ie/pages/1911/ Antrim/Belfast_East/Alexander/143235/

143 Thomas Trotter later changed sides in November 1921 when he was co-opted as a 'Labour' Unionist to the Enniskillen Urban Council by the Unionists in place of Councillor Gordon, a long-standing Nationalist Councillor, *Fermanagh Herald*, 12 November 1921.

144 *Fermanagh Times*, 8 January 1920.

145 www.census.nationalarchives.ie

146 Bureau of Military History, WS Ref # 654, Witness: Francis O'Duffy, Captain IV, Enniskillen.

147 *Fermanagh Herald*, 24 January1920.

148 *Impartial Reporter*, 7 January 1920.

149 *Fermanagh Herald*, 10 January 1920.

150 *Fermanagh Herald*, 24 January 1920.

151 *Impartial Reporter*, 9 January 1920.

152  *Impartial Reporter*, 16 January 1920.
153  *Fermanagh Times*, 4 March 1920.
154  Clarkson, *op. cit.*, pp. 298-300.
155  *Fermanagh Herald*, 8 May 1920.
156  *Fermanagh Herald*, 8 May 1920.
157  *Fermanagh Herald*, 24 May 1920.
158  *Fermanagh Herald*, 15 May 1920.
159  Patterson, *op. cit.*, pp 115-142
160  *Fermanagh Herald*, 15 January,1921.
161  *Fermanagh Herald*, 9 July 1921.
162  Walker, *op. cit.*, p.19
163  *Fermanagh Herald*, 28 August 1920.
164  *Fermanagh Herald*, 12 February 1921.
165  *Fermanagh Herald*, 19 February 1921.
166  *Fermanagh Herald*, 6 August 1921.
167  *Fermanagh Herald*, 5 November 1921.
168  *Impartial Reporter*, 15 July 1922.
169  *Fermanagh Herald*, 17 October 1931.
170  *Fermanagh Herald*, 9 September 1922.
171  *Fermanagh Herald*, 9 September 1922.
172  Board of Trade, *Labour Gazette*, June 1922, p.248.
173  Boyd, *op. cit.*, p.99.
174  Buckland, *op. cit.*, p.153.
175  Clegg, *op. cit.*, p.103.
176  Clarkson, *op. cit.*, pp.320-321.
177  Boyd, *op. cit.*, p.99.
178  *Impartial Reporter*, 10 December 1921.
179  *Fermanagh Herald*, 29 April 1922.
180  *Impartial Reporter*, 26 January 1922.
181  Walker, *op. cit.*, pp.19-20.
182  *Fermanagh Herald*, 28 January 1922.
183  *Fermanagh Herald*, 18 February 1922.
184  *Impartial Reporter*, 26 January 1922.
185  *Fermanagh Herald*, 9 September 1922.
186  TGWU, *The Story of the TGWU*, (TGWU, London, 1975). p.19.
187  *Fermanagh Herald*, 27 January,1923.
188  Clegg, *op. cit.*, pp. 103-108.
189  *Fermanagh Herald*, 3 March 1923.
190  *Fermanagh Herald*, 10 March 1923.
191  *Fermanagh Herald*, 17 March 1923.
192  *Fermanagh Herald*, 7 April 1923.
193  *Fermanagh Herald*, 12 May 1923.
194  *Fermanagh Herald*, 9 June 1923.
195  TGWU, Executive Minutes, 18 November 1923
196  *Fermanagh Herald*, 24 March 1923.
197  *Fermanagh Herald*, 14 April 1923.
198  *Fermanagh Herald*, 12 May 1923.
199  *Fermanagh Herald*, 28 April 1923.
200  *Fermanagh Herald*, 21 August 1937.
201  *Ulster Herald*, 5 August 1950
202  Irish Genealogy, Civilrecords.irishgeneaology.ie
203  Census.nationalarchives.ie
204  *Fermanagh Herald*, 1 February,1930.
205  *Fermanagh Mail*, 23 July 1890.

206 Census, nationalarchives.ie
207 Much of this chapter was published as Jim Quinn "No homes for people or books: Labour's housing struggles in Enniskillen, 1915-1932' in Byers & Devine, *William Walker, op. cit.*, pp. 157-168.
208 *Fermanagh Herald*, 17 April 1915.
209 *Fermanagh Herald*, 11 November 1919.
210 Helen Lannigan Wood, *Enniskillen: Historic Image of an Island Town*, (Friars Bush Press, 1990), p. .30. The writer began his schooling there for two years from September 1960.
211 Livingstone, *op, cit.*
212 *Fermanagh Herald*, 19 April 1919.
213 *Fermanagh Herald*, 10 May 1919.
214 *Fermanagh Herald*, 7 June 1919.
215 *Fermanagh Herald*, 23 August 1919.
216 *Fermanagh Herald*, 18 October 1919.
217 *Fermanagh Herald*, 8 May 1920.
218 *Fermanagh Herald*, 17 April 1920.
219 *Fermanagh Herald*, 23 January 1926.
220 *Fermanagh Herald*, 18 September 1926.
221 *Fermanagh Herald*, 31 October 1925.
222 *Fermanagh Herald*, 11 December 1926.
223 The Labour Party, Northern Ireland, Report of Executive Committee to the 5th Annual Conference, 31 March 1928, PRONI D3702/B/2
224 *Fermanagh Herald*, 4 June 1927.
225 *Fermanagh Herald*, 12 November 1927.
226 *Fermanagh Herald*, 19 November 1927.
227 *Fermanagh Herald*, 8 January 1927.
228 *Fermanagh Herald*, 10 March 1928.
229 *Fermanagh Herald*, 8 December 1928.
230 *Fermanagh Herald*, 12 May 1928.
231 *Fermanagh Herald*, 7 July 1928.
232 *Fermanagh Herald*, 25 August 1928.
233 Kennedy & Ollerenshaw, *op. cit.*, p. 213.
234 *Fermanagh Herald*, 7 July 1928.
235 *Fermanagh Herald*, 19 January 1929.
236 *Fermanagh Herald*, 20 April 1929.
237 Livingstone, *op, cit.*, pp. 322-333.
238 *Fermanagh Herald*, 9 February 1929.
239 *Fermanagh Herald*, 8 June 1929.
240 From 1925, the TGWU adopted the title Amalgamated TGWU in Ireland to distinguish it from the Irish TGWU formed in 1909.
241 *Fermanagh Herald*, 1 February 1930.
242 *Fermanagh Herald*, 22 March 1930.
243 *Fermanagh Herald*, 1 March 1930.
244 *Fermanagh Herald*, 3 May 1930.
245 *Fermanagh Herald*, 18 October 1930.
246 *Fermanagh Herald*, 6 December 1930.
247 *Fermanagh Herald*, 7 February 1931.
248 PRONI D/1931/114/1013/30/471
249 *Fermanagh Herald*, 2 May 1931.
250 *Fermanagh Herald*, 30 May 1931.
251 *Fermanagh Herald*, 12 September 1931.
252 *Fermanagh Herald*, 16 January 1932.
252 *Fermanagh Herald*, 7 May 1932

Fermanagh Branch NI/B3010

Proud to be celebrating 100 years of the Fermanagh Council of Trade Unions

1919-2019

*'Workers of the world unite, you have nothing to lose but your chains'*

*Meets In Fermanagh House, Enniskillen, 2nd Thursday of every month 7.30pm if you need a union*

**Mandate Trade Union – The Retail, Bar and Administrative Workers' Union**

*Sends  greetings to*

## The  Fermanagh Council of Trade Unions

*on the occasion of their centenary*

*"1919-2019"*

*We wish them well in their next  Century of Workers Progress*

**General Secretary:**                    **John Douglas**

**THE CWU NI TELECOMS BRANCH SENDS
FERMANAGH COUNCIL OF TRADE UNIONS
FRATERNAL BEST WISHES AND SUCCESS IN ITS
CENTENARY YEAR 2019**

*The communications union*
*NI Telecom Branch*

*"Justice is the goal; solidarity is the tool; education is the key!'*

*www.cwuniteb.org*

*branch@btinternet.com*

CWU Regional Office
26 – 34
Antrim Road
Belfast
BT15 2AA
02890 321771

# ASTI
A century of service

**Campaigning for:**
- **Investment in education**
- **Inclusive education**
- **Quality education**

**Connect Trade Union**

(Formerly TEEU & UCATT)

*The Executive Council extends congratulations to the*

*Fermanagh Council of Trade Unions on your 100th*

*Anniversary*

**Paddy Kavanagh, General Secretary**

www.connectunion.ie

**THE UNION FOR CRAFT AND SKILLED TECHNICAL, ENGINEERING, ELECTRICAL AND CONSTRUCTION WORKERS IN IRELAND**

 DUBLIN COUNCIL OF
TRADES UNIONS

*Extends Greetings and Best Wishes to*
*Fermanagh Council of Trade Unions*
*on the occasion of their Centenary*
*and a century of workers progress*

**President:** Betty Tyrell-Collard **Secretary:** Sam Nolan

# BRAY AND DISTRICT
# COUNCIL OF TRADE UNIONS

**Founded 1917**

*Celebrating*

**100 YEARS**

OF LEADERSHIP CONTINUITY
CAMPAIGNING AND PROGRESS

## Congratulations to Fermanagh
## on joining the 100 year club!

**Affiliated to
Irish Congress of Trade Unions**

*INTO Northern Conference 30th April 2018,*
*celebrating 150 years of INTO, 1868 – 2018,*
*Lough Erne Golf resort, Enniskillen.*

INTO was 150 years old last year (1868 – 2018). It is the longest and largest established teacher's union and the only one organised island wide. Historically, the INTO has struck a balance between the interests of the pay and conditions of its members and serving educational and by extension societal progress.

Its first president Vere Foster has been described as one whose work was characterised by a vibrant humanity and a disregard for the pretensions of class; those themes are also at the heart of the INTO's history.

INTO represents over 40,000 teachers across the island with over 7,000 members in the north across all levels and sectors.

## *INTO Congratulates the Fermanagh Council of Trade Unions in its Centenary Year and wishes the Council every success in the future*

Irish Region, Unite the Union

---

# Celebrating 100 Years

---

**Enniskillen** Trades & Labour Council
1919

**Fermanagh** Council of Trade Unions
2019

**In our unity, there is strength!**

unite
the**UNION**